A Precious Gift For You!!!

TELL OTHERS ABOUT IT. ☺
WWW.ECHOESOFHEAVEN.ORG
Email: Passion@EchoesofHeaven.org

Elephant

08/06

Echoes of Heaven
God's Love is Better Than Life Itself

Charles Elephant

Bloomington, IN Milton Keynes, UK

AuthorHouse™
1663 Liberty Drive, Suite 200
Bloomington, IN 47403
www.authorhouse.com
Phone: 1-800-839-8640

AuthorHouse™ UK Ltd.
500 Avebury Boulevard
Central Milton Keynes, MK9 2BE
www.authorhouse.co.uk
Phone: 08001974150

First published by AuthorHouse 5/8/2006
ISBN: 1-4259-2551-0 (e)
ISBN: 1-4259-2552-9 (sc)
ISBN: 1-4259-2566-9 (hc)

Printed in the United States of America
Bloomington, Indiana

This book is printed on acid-free paper.

Library of Congress Control Number: 2006902360

All scripture quotations in this publication are from the Contemporary English. Copyright © 1991, 1992, 1995 by American Bible Society. Used by permission.

Author Services Rep. :	*Crystal Yoakam:*	*Author House*
Design Consultant:	*Jenifer Brandt:*	*Author House*
Graphic Designer:	*Bridgette Swab*	*Author House*
Galley Designer:	*Lori Fender*	*Author House*
Production Editor:	*Regina Clarke:*	*WordsRU*
Copy Editor:	*Stephanee Killen:*	*Integrative Ink*
Cover designer:	*Michelle Johnson*	*Exodus Design*

DEDICATION

God, my Father, hallowed be your name. My heart is a small boat, your joy is my shore and your love is my anchor. Sweet are the promises, kind is your word, pure is your mind, forgiving and free. Sweet is the tender love you have shown to the world, particularly to me. God, you have really loved me. I was a wayward, wandering child, a slave of sin, until this blessed promise fell, the sweetest melody on my ear: "Charles, come unto me, weary and heavy-laden, for there is sweet rest for you." Oh love that would not let me go, I rest my weary soul in you. God, I drew my life from you and I give it back again, the life I owe, living for you alone. Remind me each morning of your constant love, for I put trust in you. My prayers go up to you; show me the way I should go. What else have I in heaven but you? Since I have you, what else could I want on earth? My mind and my body may grow weak, but God, you alone, is my strength; you are all I ever need.

Teach me your perfect and righteous ways, O God; make them known to me. Teach me to live according to your truth and righteousness, for you are my God, my Lord who saves me in times of trouble. I will always praise, worship, obey and trust in you, my love and caring heavenly Father. I pray to you, God, for your completeness and fullness. I came to earth with nothing, Lord, except the breath of life, and you have given me everything. For all you have blessed me, I give you praise.

May you God help me to remain in your grace, walk in your glory and also make me a mirror to reflect your love, glory, joy and peace to the world.

Amen.

ACKNOWLEDGEMENTS

This book has benefited enormously from the generous input and support of many individuals.

I owe special thanks to Sylvia Kinyanjui, Rose Kuria, Mazhar Dar, Jenell Clarke and Chandani Valiathan for your love and encouragement. Thank you for being there for me with your sweet words of hope. When I felt low you lifted me up; at a time when I thought it was a dream you brought reality into my life by telling me that everything is possible. You made me believe in myself, and gain confidence and courage, so that I could be ready to serve God with a clean and clear mind. Thanks for your support and interest in the progress of my work.

I also want to express my gratitude and appreciation for the tremendous contributions of Regina Clarke and Stephanee Killen for support of this book by editing and reviewing the manuscript for me and providing insights, comments and suggestions that helped improve its quality and readability. Special thanks go to Regina Clarke in the preparation of this book and for her thoughtful review of the manuscript. I was fortunate enough to have her help as an expert and dedicated individual who assisted me in transcribing, editing and organizing the work, and in designing the internal layout of my manuscript draft.

Special thanks go to Michelle Johnson and Kris Cotterman for the cover's graphic design. Thanks for their dedication and professional work. In addition, special thanks to the American Bible Society for all scriptures quotations, Wikimedia Common organization for the illuminated painting of Saint John on Patmos (from the Book of Hours in the Duc de Berry collection), Ross Hamilton for the green pasture picture and Free Nature Pictures for the desert picture.

Finally, special thanks are also due to Crystal Yoakam and the Author House family for their dedication to the development, design, production and distribution of this book.

PREFACE

Are you in a desert, or in green pastures?

It is in the desert we hear echoes of heaven. The desert presents opportunities to both man and God—an opportunity for God to glorify Himself by performing miracles, an opportunity for man to experience God's love and power. In green pastures, with water all around, we need no miracles. But our souls are often in the desert, and that is why we need to hear from heaven, to be able to walk with God. The desert is a meeting place for both man and God. If we do not walk across the desert every day, we cannot realize the love and favour of God. Yea, we cannot appreciate His mighty deeds.

The desert can be either a place or a state of mind. It is the literal place where God chose to reveal Himself to messengers and prophets. It is also a state of being, for you may have every material thing you desire in the world, yet inside your soul you may not feel happy or content or at peace. In that situation your soul is in the desert, and you need to find something that can make your soul satisfied again. That is when you need to seek God's guidance.

In this book I have explained what religion is. Ultimately, it is a relationship between each one of us and God. God has sent guidance to us through prophets, messengers and loved ones. They all have come before us with messages of guidance or reconciliation, telling us how to live the short life we have in this merciless and bitter world. It is our responsibility to follow God's guidance, the true religion, because we will be judged. Those who were sent by God to bring His guidance did their work and we need to do our work, too. If we claim that we are following their teachings, then they have set a standard, an example for us to follow.

What then are green pastures—what state do they reveal to us? They represent the state that exists when our soul is content and at peace. That can only be achieved through a good relationship with God, by believing, trusting, obeying and living according to His guidance. If you have peace within you, it does not matter where you are physically or what you are going through—every place, every situation is a green pasture for you because you believe in Him. Therefore, you have nothing to complain about, but rather only need to glorify and appreciate God for everything that happens in your life, knowing that God has a good purpose for you, and beyond circumstances and situations there is peace, which exists in the green pastures.

When you are in the desert, you are all alone, desperate and confused because you cannot trace your direction and you can find nothing to eat or drink. That is when you need to call upon the name of God, and He will answer you. Seek for His guidance and He will guide you. When you follow His guidance, you are walking with Him and your soul will be at peace.

Green pastures do not represent material prosperity, but spiritual prosperity. Material prosperity does not give peace; it only creates the illusion of green pastures, a mirage in the middle of the desert. We came into this world with nothing and we will leave it with nothing except our deeds and actions, good or bad, that will follow us. Spiritual prosperity or peace comes from the creator of the universe, our heavenly loving and caring Father, our Lord God. We all need to be in green pastures, not in the desert.

God created Adam and Eve and placed them in the Garden of Eden, a place filled with green pastures. When they ran short of God's glory, they were chastened and sent away from the Garden of Eden and went to wander in the desert. Ever since, we have all been born in the desert as a state of mind, and we live there until we ask God to send our soul back into the Garden of Eden again. When we run short of God's glory because of our sins, this automatically sends us back into the desert. When we approach or call upon the name of God for guidance with a true and sincere, repentant heart, through His mercy, grace and love He answers and forgives us. Repentance and forgiveness carry us back to the green pastures and into God's loving shelter.

Trust in God at all times, the children of he Most High God. Tell Him all your troubles, for He is our refuge. Remember we are like a puff of breath; great and small, rich and poor alike are worthless. But it is better to obey God than to sacrifice the best sheep to Him. Rebellion against Him is as bad of witch craft and arrogance is as sinful as idolatry.

Peace, joy and happiness come from God only through good relationship but we cannot buy them. Giving and helping others without having a good relationship with Him first does not give them either.

For those who trust, obey and wait upon the Lord God

will dwell in the green pastures all their lives.

TABLE OF CONTENTS

PART I

CHAPTER 1

SONGS OF PRAISE

This chapter is written to praise, worship and adore God before encountering the rest of the book. It helps one to prepare and understand the content that follows. It is good to praise and worship God because He is good and worthy of our devotion every moment. This is a devotion that does not apply to a particular religion but to everything that has life today. It is my humble prayer to God, the creator of the universe, that as you read through this book He will bless you with peace, joy and understanding.

Psalm 145: A Hymn of Praise

I will proclaim your greatness, my God and king; I will thank you forever and ever. Every day I will thank you; I will praise you forever and ever. The Lord is great and meant to be highly praised; for His greatness is beyond understanding.

What you have done, my God, will be praised from one generation to the next; they will proclaim your mighty acts. They will speak of your glory and majesty, and I will meditate on your wonderful deeds. People will speak of your mighty deeds, and I will tell them about all your greatness and sing about your kindness.

For the Lord is loving and merciful, slow to become angry and full of constant love. He is good to everyone and has compassion on all He has made.

All your creatures, Lord, will praise you, and all your people will give you thanks. They will speak of the glory of your royal power and tell of your might, so that everyone will know your mighty deeds and the glorious majesty of your kingdom. Your rule is eternal, and you are king forever.

The Lord is faithful to His promises, and everything He does is good. He helps those who are in trouble; He lifts those who have fallen.

All living things look hopefully to you, and you give them food when they need it. You give them enough and satisfy the needs of all.

The Lord is righteous in all He does, merciful in all His acts. He is near to those who call to Him, who call to Him with sincerity. He supplies the needs of those who honour Him; He hears their cries and saves them. He protects everyone who loves Him, but He will destroy the wicked. I will always praise the Lord; let all His creatures praise His holy name forever.

Psalm 103: Love of God

Praise the Lord, my soul! All my being, praise His holy name! Praise the Lord, my soul, and do not forget how kind He is. He forgives all my sins and heals all my diseases. He keeps me from the grave and blesses me with love and mercy. He fills my life with good things, so that I stay young and strong like an eagle. The Lord judges in favour of the oppressed and gives them their rights. He revealed His plans to me and has let the people of the world see his mighty deeds.

The Lord is merciful and loving, slow to become angry and full of constant love. He does not keep on rebuking; He is not angry forever. He does not punish us as we deserve or repay us for our sins and wrongs. As high as the sky is above the earth, so great is His love for those who honour Him. As far as the east is from the west, so far does He remove our sins from us. As kind as a father is to his children, so kind is the Lord to those who honour Him. He knows what we are made of; He remembers that we are dust.

As for us, our life is like grass. We grow and flourish like a wildflower; then the wind blows on it, and it is gone—no one sees it again. But for those who honour the Lord, His love lasts forever, and His goodness endures for all generations of those who are true to His covenant and who faithfully obey His commands. The Lord placed His throne in heaven; He is king over all. Praise the Lord, you strong and mighty angels, who obey His commands, who listen to what He says. Praise the Lord, all you heavenly powers, you servants of His, who do His will! Praise the Lord, all His creatures in all the places He rules. Praise the Lord, my soul!

Psalm 138

I thank you, Lord, with all my heart; I sing praise to you before the gods. I face your holy temple, bow down, and praise your name because of your constant love and faithfulness, because you have shown that your name and your commands are supreme. You answered me when I called to you; with your strength you strengthened me.

All the kings in the world will praise you, Lord, because they have heard your promises. They will sing about what you have done and about your great glory. Even though you are so high above, you care for the lowly, and the proud cannot hide from you. When I am surrounded by troubles, you keep me safe. You oppose my angry enemies and save me by your power. You do everything you have promised; Lord, your love is eternal. Complete the work that you have begun.

Psalm 147

It is good to sing praise to our God; it is pleasant and right to praise Him. The Lord is restoring my heart; He is bringing back what has been stolen from me. He heals the broken-hearted and bandages their wounds. He has decided the number of the stars and calls each one by name. Great and mighty is our Lord; His wisdom cannot be measured. He raises the humble, but crushes the wicked to the ground. Sing hymns of praise to the Lord; play music on the harp to our God. He spreads clouds over the sky; He provides rain for the earth and makes grass grow on the hills. He gives animals their food and feeds the young ravens when they call. His pleasure is neither in strong horses, nor His delight in brave soldiers; but He takes pleasure in those who honour Him, in those who trust in His constant love. Praise the Lord, O my heart! Praise your God, O my heart! He has lifted you up from the dust; He keeps on renewing your strength every day. He keeps your borders safe and satisfies you with the finest wheat.

He gives a command to the earth, and what He says is quickly done. He spreads snow like a blanket and scatters frost like dust. He sends hail like gravel; no one can endure the cold He sends! Then He gives a command, and the ice melts; He sends the wind, and the water flows. He gives messages to me, His instructions and laws to my heart. He has not done this for other people; they do not know his laws. Praise the Lord!

CHAPTER 2

INTRODUCTION

Since I came to know God and understand His ways, my life has been changed. At first, I was confused and bothered because I could not understand myself, and my life seemed nothing but chaos. I was tired of hearing the same scriptures being read in the church, such as the story of the prodigal son, or the stories of Abraham, Isaac, and Moses, among others. Every day I used to wonder, *Where is God?... for nowadays He does not speak to us.* I wanted to hear directly from God and learn more from Him. I knew that if there was a God, surely He had good stories to tell me. I longed for those good stories day and night until finally God heard my prayers and blessed me according to my heart's desire.

To begin, my parents are Mr. Johnson Njogu Muthuu and Mrs. Lear Wairimu Njogu. My parents have eight children—two sons and six daughters. The last two children were twins, a boy and a girl, and I happened to be one of them. I was born and brought up in a small town called Mukurwei-ini in Nyeri, Kenya. Later I moved to Nairobi, the capital city of Kenya.

First, I would like to express my sincere gratitude to my parents, due to the love they have given to me, my brother, my sisters, and my extended family. It has been a blessing to be a member of the family, and I have truly appreciated their presence in my life. My life has not been normal since childhood. Therefore, my family should not regret anything that they have done to me. I am proud of them for the tremendous contributions they have made in my life, consciously or unconsciously. The rejections that I received were for a better life because they opened my eyes to God and to understanding His will. They drew me closer to His grace, and my eyes were opened to see the glory and wonders of God.

If I had been well-received and well-treated by the family, surely I could not have walked with God in my life. Therefore, they should be proud because God has used them in one way or the other to mold and prepare me for His mission.

As I write about my encounter with God, I do not hold a grudge with anyone. In fact, I pray and give thanks to the almighty God for everyone in my family. My words to them are these: *Do not forget that God has a good plan for you, and remember Jesus loves you all. I appreciate the wonderful times we had together. I urge you to seek God enthusiastically because He loves you, and He will never fail or forsake you, no matter what may come. God has given you this opportunity to repent your sins, to turn back to Him; failure to do so means that you will perish and be forgotten when the day of the Lord comes.*

I would like to reveal to all my relatives and friends that when I met God, I had nothing valuable to give to Him. The only thing I had was myself. I donated my life to Him for His glory. This means that I sacrificed my interests by surrendering my entire life to be used as a vessel, a digging hoe, or a golden shepherd's rod by the Most High God. He accepted my sacrifice and offered to cleanse me for His work. That is why I have not yet started a family—because I made a commitment to my God. But if it is the will of God, I will have one. My purpose is to do what God sent me to do, because the night is coming. It is true that some are born for the kingdom of God and others for the earthly kingdom. This means that there are those who were born for the purpose of filling the world and others for the purpose of filling heaven. I am proud of the decision because I know God is alive, and He will reward me according to the richness of His kingdom.

The reason for writing this chronicle is because believing comes through hearing, seeing, touching, or using other senses. My main reason is to introduce to all mankind the simple way to build a good relationship with God. I want people to know that there is a living God of the universe whose name is Jehovah, and Jesus Christ, the savior of mankind, is alive, too. He suffered, died on the cross, and was resurrected so that we could possess the kingdom of God. None of you need go through the process that I went through in order to believe, because it is a very long and time-consuming process. All that I want you to understand is that God has good plans for you, and Jesus loves you to such an extent that he sacrificed his own life for you and me.

It is important to grow and increase the relationship between you and God. Know the purpose that God has for you, because we are all called for a celestial mission. It was not an accident that you came into this world. No matter who you are or what you go through, remember that God loves you and knows you by your name. No situation or circumstance should hinder you from touching the heart of God. The important point to note is how to praise and glorify the loving and caring heavenly Father while you live in this world. You should understand that the past should not steal your future, but rather should illuminate the future and help you develop new ways of handling future challenges. Heaven is a destination for us all.

Each day has its own life—the sun rises to welcome a newborn day, and as the sun passes across the sky, the day grows old; the sun sets and the day dies peacefully, giving way to another day to be born. Life is a long road of cleansing ourselves to be able to see God. This means that each day marks the beginning and end of new life for you. Although the world is full of suffering, it is also full of overcoming our challenges through Jesus Christ. Many people have faced challenges in their lives but found solutions through trusting in God. It is important to look beyond the obstacles and the world in which we live. Even if the road is paved with tears and bitterness, God will prevail by achieving the impossible. He will pave the road with blessings, joy, and the peace that comes from Him. He is a loving and caring God ready to lead you home. Across the river of Jordan, the river of death, there will be no tears, no suffering, no sickness, no oppression, no death, and God is waiting to wipe your tears and to heal your broken heart.

One major problem is that we live tomorrow's life, but not today's. God is simple and made life very simple for all of us, though we try to complicate it so much. It is easy to experience the presence of God and to feel the warmth of His heart, if only we live one day at a time. Remember that God loves you; therefore, let His joy be your strength every day—let the sun shine on your face. Do not look behind you or to the side; God is calling you with a tender heart to hold your hand in order to lead you in the righteous way. He wants to go before you, and you should follow Him.

My dear friend, you need to understand the simple fact that you came into this world alone, you are all alone no matter how many people surround you, and you will leave this world alone. Your relatives, friends, acquaintances, and other members of your community cannot understand your suffering, though they may comfort you with sweet words. No one can understand another's pain because such suffering cannot be shared. Even at your time of death, those who will surround you will tell you that they understand, but they will not have tasted death, and they will not be ready to share death with you. In fact, if you request a volunteer, someone who would be willing to take your suffering or death on your behalf, no one would step forward. Sincerely speaking, that is the time when you will know that you are all alone. People will offer you prayers, flowers, and thoughts, but they will leave you with your Creator. You came from Him and to Him you will return. Glory be to His Holy name. In other words, no one loves or cares for you as they claim. Most of them will come to witness that you are leaving. That is why God offered Jesus as a sacrifice to the world, to share our suffering by carrying the burden of our sins.

Today, God wants you to come back to Him, to be His loved one, to allow Him to be a part of your heart so that He can become a part of you. He will be your best friend, and even at the time of death, He will be with you to lead you home. You will never be alone again; you will be walking with your loving Father. His name is Jehovah, God, the creator of the universe. Troubles and problems will not leave you, but you will not face them alone. You will go through serious troubles and problems, such as a deadly sickness, but God will command them to leave you instantly. You will go through fire, but He will order the fire not to harm you. You will be involved in an accident, but He will hold you safely with His precious hands and you will escape unhurt. Floods will draw you, but He will order the water to dry up or hold your right hand and save you. You will be cornered by your enemies, and He will stretch out His precious hands to cradle you. You will be discouraged and disappointed, but God will give you hope, encouragement, and lift you up. The enemies will besiege you, but they will disappear in seven ways. You will be weary and tedious, but God will refresh and renew your strength because he will be the source of your strength. Your enemies and wild animals will be behind you, ready to attack you, but glory to God, He will lift you up from the midst of all these and save you. His hand will attract you like a magnet and lift you up to the sky, and your enemies will be left in despair looking high above. He creates a way where there is no way, because He is God. Turn to Him today, and you will live and enjoy walking in his presence.

We all like to be loved because it makes us feel secure. But we fear rejection from those we love. Rejection makes one feel worthless, discouraged, and useless. God is a loving and caring Father. No matter who we are or what we have done, He is ready to open His precious arms to welcome us back into His kingdom with love. God does not condemn or reject any repentant heart. Do not fear to come to God because He will not reject you. He is not like human beings and that is why He is God. He loves you just the way you are. You are wonderfully made in the image of God. The sins that you have committed in the past do not matter to God if only you turn back to Him. He will cleanse you and dress you in kingly style. The greatest sin of all is not to accept Him in our hearts. There should be no condemnation of the house of God.

Before I met God, I was desperate; I hated myself because I had no hope, and my life was nothing but misery. Since I met God, and we agreed to walk together, my life has completely changed. He gave me hope and the love that I had not found from anyone in this merciless and bitter world. I was dying to hear someone whisper, "I love you," but no one ever did. When I met God was the first time I heard those words. At first, I was amazed and confused because I could not understand why God loved me when no one else would. Today, I do not care what people say, but I care about hearing God repeat those magic words. He gave me the true meaning of life. He gave me a new beginning without end because He said He is Alpha and Omega, the Beginning and the End.

That is why I feel obliged to extend the same care and love to everyone who crosses my path. I believe everyone in this world wants to hear those loving words, though most of the time they are misused. Therefore, my dear brother and sister, remember that God loves you as a person, and I do, too.

CHAPTER 3

GOD'S CALLING

This chapter explores the calling of God. It is a long process; most of the time we need to understand things after they have taken place. My problems and the suffering that I went through were not unique, and I believe many go through situations far worse than mine. But the reason to include them in this book is because they were calls of awakening. Through suffering we are able to look or wait upon the Lord. I pray that for those who are going through problems and suffering today, God gives them strength to persevere until they experience victory. But God calls us, awakens us, in different ways. No matter what situations we are in today, God is still faithful to us.

To start with, I would like to apologize because the best I can do is to narrate my own encounters, Yet, I will touch upon the most relevant instances I believe can be helpful to you in building your relationship with God. Every day is a day of miracles and new learning. I cannot put everything in writing, but you can learn more directly from God. I can only give you about forty percent of what God has revealed, but the rest may come through interaction, through asking questions, through emails, and through letters. You may choose to disagree with my experiences because it is hard to dream my dreams. In this, I would then urge you to ask God for more revelation or clarification for your own self. I am not claiming that I am more righteous, only that it was through God's grace and favor that I was made holy again.

I began to seek the truth because I knew the truth was out there. I wanted to know God and understand His ways in a simple manner, taught by Him. I refused to accept or believe based on ancient stories unless God proved to me that those stories were true. To me, a Bible was nothing more than myth if God could not prove His word to me. I also wondered whether God had perhaps existed a long time ago but had left and abandoned the world.

I was brought up in a Christian family and used to attend a Greek Orthodox Church (Thunguri) back home in Nyeri, Kenya. My mom offered me in the church through the priest, Father Peter Kinyua, at the age of about seven, and after that I became an altar boy. My major responsibility was to take care of the altar, lighting pulpit candles, opening the church on Sunday morning for the service, and helping the father (priest) while conducting the church services.

One Sunday morning around 9 a.m., as I was alone in the course of my duties cleaning and sweeping the pulpit, I heard the sounds of a mass choir coming from the floor. This was very surprising to me, as the church was isolated, and we had no audio devices like a radio or television set. I opened the door to check outside. I went around the building, but found no one. Because I was bold and eager, I went back into the church without fear. When I went back, I did not hear the voices again, but I was convinced that they had been the voices of angels, because the sound had been a combination of sweet melody without words or instruments. I did not share this story with anyone because no one would have believed me. This event took place when I was about nine years of age.

It was my duty every evening around 6 p.m. to get some milk from a neighbor who lived about three kilometers from our house. On my way home, I had to pass through a stadium. As a young boy, I used to play with other kids up until 7 p.m. before going to get milk. Sometimes I used to go very late, and my mom complained, but as a boy, I did not care. One evening, as usual, I went for milk. It was dark as I headed back home. Although there was moonlight, I could hardly recognize someone from a distance. As I started walking across the stadium, I saw two people in front of me who appeared to be heading in the direction I was heading. They were wearing white clothes. I ran after them, but they ran, too. All the time, the distance between us remained constant, until, after reaching the other end of the stadium, they vanished. I went home amazed and frightened, but I did not share this with anyone. After that, I would receive revelations of events, like a death in the village, but I never used to share this with anyone because I thought people would call me a witch and kill me.

During that time, my dad and mom started having domestic problems. Being the youngest of three kids in the family, we bore the burden of the consequences. I became the main target or victim. Sometimes we would be left alone to take care of ourselves. I loved my mom so much, and I could feel and see her suffering. I could play with other kids during the day, but mourning and tears were the order of the nights. During that time, I could ask God many questions, but I received no answer.

My twin sister and I completed our primary education and passed. We were admitted to two separate high schools. That was when my real life encounters began. My father took my sister to a boarding school away from home so that she would not be disturbed or disrupted. When he came back home, I asked him about my school, which I was supposed to join a week later, but he confessed to me that he had no business with my education whatsoever. In fact, he said, "the child I was taking to school is in school, and the one I am not paying for is at home. Tell your mom to take you to the school of her choice." I told my mom, and I cried bitterly throughout the night, calling upon the Holy name of the Lord because I knew it was the end of my dreams. My mom had no money, since she was a housewife, and she and my father were not on good terms. In fact, their marriage had died a long time ago, but no one was ready to bury it.

My brother was scheduled to come home that weekend, and my mom requested that he pay for my school fees. Unfortunately, he was not prepared to take on that burden, and therefore agreed with my mom that he would take me to a nearby boarding/day school about eight kilometers away from home.

When a student enters high school, it is supposed to be a moment of joy. The boys go through initiation ceremonies from childhood to manhood. It is an organized event. For me, I had to trust God in everything. In fact, I did not inform anyone except my twin sister about my initiation. I borrowed money from my twin sister and went to the hospital very early in the morning to be circumcised. A friend took me, and we had to go to a hospital far away so that by the time my parents came to know about it, everything would have been done. We came back home and met my mom on her way to a shopping center, and I told her because I knew the operation could not be reversed.

The rest of the family only learned about this later, because that was the only way to avoid confrontation and curses from my parents. The candidates were also getting gifts of new clothes and shoes, among other things. To me, it was a moment of sadness. The only new items I received included a Bible, an English Dictionary, and a Geometrical set. I had no shoes to put on, and the only pair I could use belonged to my older sister. Students were laughing at me because I was wearing a girl's shoes, but the only way out was to become hardcore or indifferent. Sometimes it might rain heavily in the morning, and I did not have a raincoat, umbrella, or gumboots.

By this time, I was no longer committed to God's will. I attended church services irregularly, though I still trusted in Him so much. Sometimes I could even convince my friends to attend church services because I argued that God had a favorite child, to whom He had made a promise that He would always do whatever that child asked of Him. Perhaps that child was one of us, I would say to them. Therefore, it was a good idea to attend the service in order to release blessings for the congregation.

During my high school life, several events took place. One night I was sleeping and I had a dream inside a dream. I was dreaming of being asleep and having another dream. The dream inside a dream was about the end of the world. The world was divided in half: one side belonged to God, and the other side belonged to the Devil. In that connection, I saw myself being rejected by God and the Devil both. Therefore, since I did not belong to any kingdom, I became a messenger.

After I woke from the dream, I was bothered. I used to tell my friends not to follow me because God and the Devil would reject me, and I would have a special place between heaven and hell all on my own. What worried me was that I could not understand why, out of billions of people, I was the only one who could not be accepted into either kingdom. But as a young person, I tried to ignore this and continue on with my normal life.

Then, after about a year, while still in high school, I had another dream. This time it was about the end of the world. Two worlds appeared. One belonged to the people and the other one belonged to God. There was a very big, deep, and dark valley that separated both worlds. The world that belonged to us was full of darkness, but God's world was bright and full of glorious light. No one was allowed to go to God's world except me. I could go to get food and drink from God's world to feed people in our world. In that dream, I heard a voice telling me that, "You are the one I have chosen to feed and take care of my people." I woke up from my dream frightened, as usual, but decided to ignore it and continue with my normal life as if nothing had happened.

First Miracle

The third event was a miracle that shocked me. At that time, our home was no longer home because there was no love or peace in it at all. Everyone went his or her own way, and I decided to deal with the problem once and for all. One Saturday morning, my father told me to cook the chicken that had been sick because people believed chickens had no serious diseases. I knew no one else in the family would agree to eat meat from a sick chicken, and therefore it was an opportunity for me to do what I wanted to do. He prepared the chicken and gave it to me to cook for him, and then he went away for some time.

After the chicken was ready, I knelt down to pray, and here was my prayer: *Jehovah God, I know you forbid us to kill, but this time I want to make my intention well known to you. To make my case, when Moses came from Mt. Sinai with the Ten Commandments and found your children doing what was evil in your eyes, he divided them into two groups, the righteous on one side, and the outrageous on the other side. He commanded the righteous to kill those who had disgraced your holy name. To me it seems that he did that in order to remove the rotten or decayed potatoes from the sack to prevent them from spreading the disease to others. Therefore, it is better for me to go to hell and save the lives of the other members of the family rather than for me to go to heaven and the rest to hell. I have offered and sacrificed myself to go to hell, and the rest of the family to join you in heaven. But if you send me to hell, then make sure you send Moses with me, too, because I am doing exactly what he did.*

I sprinkled powdered rat poison on the chicken meat and covered it well. Then I concluded my prayers by saying, *If, God, you do not want this to happen, then you have the power to prevent it. I want a miracle to happen, whereby you will send your fire to consume the meat before my father eats it; otherwise, so be your will. . . . Amen.*

I went to visit my friend, Sammy, but ready to come home in the evening prepared for the bad news. I was afraid, because I did not know exactly how the situation would turn out. After arriving home, my father was very angry with me and was not ready to listen to any explanation. He asked me where had I put the chicken meat because, although he'd found a cooking pot, well covered, it had nothing in it. In fact, there was no sign at all to indicate that I had used that pot to cook the chicken meat. To my surprise, the pot was completely clean, and I could not believe my eyes. There was no sign of cooked meat anywhere, and I definitely knew a miracle had happened!

My dad concluded that because I hated him, I had decided to throw the chicken to the dogs. He did not beat me because God was with me, though I only narrowly escaped. What happened to the chicken meat remains a mystery to me even now, but I concluded that God prevented the worst from happening because it was not His will. After that, I promised God that I would never try such a thing again, but that I would wait for His mercy and grace to save us one day.

After a couple of days, God spoke to me in a dream and told me that no one has the authority to kill another, no matter what. That was one of the basic reasons why Moses had been denied the chance to go to the land of Canaan. He had been holding the commandment that says "Thou Shall Not Kill," and he went ahead with killing all those people. But Moses had the authority and was above the commandment because God had made him to be like him and to act on his behalf. He was acting on behalf of Jehovah God almighty.

In August 1987, during the school holiday, something strange happened. It was during that time that the Catholic Church followers from my area were asserting that the Virgin Mary (the mother of Jesus) was appearing on the calendar and on oil lamps. One evening, we decided to visit the house where she was appearing because it was not far from home. We went there, and people started worshipping and praising her. Then all at once, they started pointing at the calendar, stressing that an image of Mary was appearing. I tried to focus my eyes, even changing position, but I could see nothing. I innocently said that I could not see anything. Everyone else, including my friends, Mary and Sammy, were rejoicing, but I could not understand what was wrong with me. After trying several times to see what people were seeing, I failed completely to see anything; hence, all those who were there concluded that I was a sinner and that I should go home and repent my sins first.

I was so humiliated, discouraged, and disappointed. I went back home with a lot of questions. I was very much disturbed, bearing in mind the dream that I had had some time back about being rejected by God and the Devil, too. I knew it was true that I belonged to no kingdom, and that worried me because I could not understand why I deserved that from God.

It was during the same night, as I was half-asleep, that God appeared to me. The room was filled with a bright light and heat. Then I heard a soft voice that told me not to worry because none of the people who had been at the house that night had seen anything. They believed what they wanted to believe and saw what they wanted to see. To mark the words, I was told to ask my friends individually to describe exactly what they had seen. The voice continued telling me that when Jesus comes again, every eye shall see Him whether sinner or righteous, and the Virgin Mary, too. God does not discriminate because of our sins, but a day is coming when the good shall be separated from the evil. Until this day comes, His grace and favor is sufficient for everyone who is ready to receive. *His love is unconditional to us all.*

The following day, I went to one of my friends and asked her to explain to me exactly what she had seen. To my surprise, she told me that she had not seen anything, but she'd had to concur with the group so she would not be humiliated. Later in the day, I met with another friend, and I asked him to explain, too. He said the same thing. I was content with the answers they gave and believed without doubt that it was true that God had comforted me. I thanked God because He could understand my struggle and what I was going through.

CHAPTER 4

GOD APPEARED IN PERSON

This chapter is about how I welcomed God at home without knowing it. It is true that we should love anyone who crosses our path unconditionally, because we do not know when angels might pay a courtesy visit to us. It is wrong to discriminate against others because we do not know them, or because we think they are not good-looking, or because of their color, religion, creed, sex, or age, among other things. God's love is unconditional to us all and we should give it freely and unconditionally to everyone we encounter.

That same year, in December, after completion of the fourth forms, a major and unforgettable event took place. It was a cloudless, fine evening around 8 p.m., and the full moon was high in the sky. My cousin Ben and his friend had come earlier to visit us, and I had to escort them home for about three kilometers. We decided to use the firm, muddy road (driveway) instead of the main seasonal road because there was moonlight all over, though there was a thick bush along the firm road up to where it joined the main road. I escorted them up to the Mukurwe-ini shopping center, and then I went back alone. I decided to pass through the same firm road because it was shorter. As soon as I walked half the distance, I heard a strange sound (a roaring) from the bush. I became frightened, my hair stood up, and I ran for safety. It took me less than a minute to reach the gate of our home.

Before entering the home compound, I decided to go back and see exactly what was happening, but I was prepared, ready to fly in case of any danger. I went back swiftly and listened carefully. At that time, I was able to recognize the strange sound as the sound of someone who had difficulty breathing. I courageously asked out loud whether it was a person or an animal. The sound died, and now I was ready for anything. I asked three times, and the third time a man responded in a low voice. "I am the one," he said. I asked him to identify himself, and he told me that he was from Nyahururu in Kenya about one hundred and fifty kilometers away. He had come to attend the burial of his sister, but he had gotten lost. To the best of my knowledge, there was no funeral in that area. To my surprise, my friend did not know the name of his sister's husband or any other member of the family where his sister was married. The issue became complicated because I could not figure out how to help him. He told me that he had been in the bush since 6 p.m. I told him that the best help I could offer to him was to take him to the police station to spend the night because it was safe and maybe they could help him the next day. I knew that if he refused to go to the police station with me, then he was a bad person. I could not take him home because my mom was very tough, and she would have disciplined me.

My friend came out of the bush holding a stick. What shocked me was the way he looked. He had no shoes, his shirt had no buttons, his trousers (pants) were torn, his hair was long and shaggy, and his eyes were completely red. I did not dare to look straight into his eyes. We went to the police station about three kilometers away because it was all the way back to the shopping center. All along, we kept a distance of three meters apart. He was breathing like someone who was suffering from pneumonia, and I suggested that after he went to the police station, he should go to the hospital to get treatment, and he agreed.

We went to the police station, and I explained how I had found him so that he could not be mistaken for a criminal. I explained to the policeman on duty about the incident, and he told me to show him to the hospital because it was just nearby. The man was advised to go back to the police station after treatment. Before I said goodbye, I gave him about Kshs. 5 for breakfast in the morning.

It was past 10 p.m., and the kiosks were closed. I showed him to the hospital and went on my way back home, running fearfully. I found that everyone at home was asleep; I took my dinner and went to sleep, too.

The following morning it was a sunny day and the sky was blue. At around 10 a.m. I was washing my clothes outside while narrating the whole story to my twin sister, Beatrice. Before I finished the story, I saw the same person on the main road walking down the hill. I was shocked and stopped narrating the story to watch him. He came down the hill towards our house, and as soon as he was directly facing our house, he sat down by the edge of the road. I told my sister that I must go and find out what happened at the police station. I took two gallon containers, as if I was going to fetch some water from the river. I reached the place where he was seated, and then I asked him who he was and where he was going, without identifying myself. He told me the whole story about how he had been found by a person, who had taken him to the police station, but he could not tell where he had been found. I pitied him and welcomed him home because my mom was not there. I told him that I was the person who had found him the previous night.

We went home, and my sister gave him tea and slices of bread for breakfast. Later, she made lunch for us. I asked him about his experience at the police station, and he said that it had been okay, though cold since there had been no blanket to cover him. He also told me that he did not go to the hospital. Right after I left him, he went back to the police station.

Meanwhile, I gave him water to bathe, washed his clothes, and gave him a pair of my trousers, some slippers, and a shirt with buttons. He needed Kshs.40 to go back home, and I had only Kshs.20. I borrowed Kshs.10 from my twin sister, and I went to my cousin (the one I had escorted the previous night) and explained the whole story to him. I requested him to give me Kshs.10. I went back home, and then escorted my friend to the Kiahungu bus stop. He boarded the matatu (passengers' vehicle) to Nyahururu. I paid the full bus fare, and then I went back home.

Since then, I have never heard from him, though I gave him my contact information in order to communicate later. Some time back, after I had established a good relationship with God, I asked Him why I had gained favor in his eyes and why He was so concerned about me. He said to me, "Charles, you remember the person you met in the bush—and you gave him love and care? It was me who was in him. I had come in the form of a person, and since you welcomed me, though you did not have your own place, you tried your level best to make me comfortable. You did not have enough money, but you borrowed for my sake. That is why I welcomed you in my Holy Place." This made me cry fearfully but cheerfully, knowing that I had done what was right in the eyes of God.

CHAPTER 5

GOD REVEALED HIMSELF TO ME

This chapter about how my suffering lead me to the grace and favor of God. It opened my ears to hear the echoes of heaven and my eyes to see the Glory of God in its fullness. It was not easy for me because there was a natural force that was acting directly on me. God is faithful and loving Father; He leads us step-by-step to His grace and favor. He does not allow temptations that we cannot handle. Sometime we tend to think God hates us but he is watching us no matter what we go through. He is ready to save us, if only we answer His call or call upon His Holy name. He wants to take you to another level so that you can be given a new name, the child of the Most High God, the child in the glory of God and God's love.

In 1988, I had to move to Nairobi to join a college and search for a job. This was the year that I actually met God face-to-face, though it was not fun. It took me about one year to experience what I went through, but to me it felt more like ten years. It was the year of tears and sadness. I used to cry throughout the night and grieve during the day. After I went to Nairobi, I had to stay with my brother, and my twin sister was staying with one of our elder sisters. My twin sister's education was paid for, but I had to look for casual work first to make enough money to go to college.

In Kenya, getting any job, including casual work, during those years was a nightmare. Everyone in the family frustrated me because they refused to pay for my college, and they accused me of refusing to work. I managed to get a job with a packaging company as a turn boy to ferry empty cartons or boxes from the factory to other companies. I was paid Kshs15 per day for five days. The money I was making was not enough to save for college and meet my expenses. I was disheartened because no one was there to listen to me or to understand me. Everybody turned against me, and my whole life was miserable. At that time, I was sharing a room with my nephew, though I was still under my older brother's care.

One day, God revealed to me that our mom was planning a surprise visit to Nairobi in two weeks' time. I was given the date, the time, and even the attire she would be wearing in my dream. I did not tell anyone, because I knew they would think that I was crazy. When that day came, we went to work as usual, and in the evening, I was the last one to arrive home. My mom went to my brother's place of work and later went home with my brother and his workmate. I greeted them all and sat down. Then my mom asked me why I was not excited to see her. I replied to her jokingly that I had known about her visit two weeks ago, and therefore it was not a surprise to me. My brother became furious and even declared war with me. He did not give me a chance to explain how I had known about my mom's visit. In fact, our mom tried to calm down the situation, saying that she had not told anyone about her coming, but my brother would not listen. She concluded that I was just joking because how could I have known about her visit without being told? I just kept quiet, though my brother continued to express his anger.

To me, declaring war or not had no meaning because life had no meaning to me. Actually, if there had been people I could have paid to take away my life, I would have done so. It was like telling someone who is seriously sick that he is going to fall sick.

Then, after about three and a half months, I got a job with a shoe company as a shoe trimmer. I was to apply glue on palm shoes to stick them together, but the pay was the same Kshs.15. I started sniffing glue because it was plentiful, but a few weeks later, I experienced the side effects. My gums started breeding, and I became nervous and emotional.

At this stage, I was completely hopeless, and my life was full of fear, loneliness, and desperation. I knew my life was over, and I longed for death to come because it was the only solution I had. My prayers were not to see the next day, week, month, or year because I had no future. I was only praying that God would enable me to see the glory of the sunrise and in the evening to see the glory of the sunset. The future had no meaning to me because the best it had for me was bitterness, misery, and sadness. My heart was ailing. I was longing for God and waiting patiently for Him to take me home because I was tired of living, but He never appeared. I thought it was wise to be specific in my prayers and to approach God with a sincere heart. This time I changed my prayers, and this is what I prayed:

Oh God, the Creator of the universe and all its inheritance, I humble myself before you to give thanks and to request something special. First, I would like to thank you for those years you have blessed me to see the sunrises and sunsets, but I am humbly requesting you to take me home. I cannot blame you for anything that has fallen upon me because some of us were meant to suffer and others to enjoy, but now I am eager and willing to come home. Father, according to the gospel of Jesus, he promised that whoever will knock it shall be opened, whatever we pray with a sincere heart, you shall provide, and Jesus further clarified to us that no child asks his father for bread, only to have the father gives him a stone, or asks for a fish, only to receive a snake. Then you, being my heavenly Father, must bless me according to my heart's desire. Today I approach your throne with a sincere heart, praying for death (it is my bread or fish now). In giving me life, you are giving me a stone or a snake. My dear heavenly Father, do I deserve to get what I have not asked for? I know and believe I do not deserve to approach your throne, but please, my dear heavenly Father, if you can do me a favor and give me what I have requested, I will gratify your Holy name on my way home to heaven. Lord, be kind to your son and meet his heart's desire. Your son, Charles Elephant, is waiting anxiously to die. Amen."

God never responded to my request.

God refused to give me what I prayed for. After some time, repeating the same prayer for several days, I grew impatient. One time I told Him that if He could not take away my life, I would do it. At that time, I was longing to meet death by opening the door for a murderer to come my way and kill me. I tried to open doors for death to come, but all in vain.

One day, I made up my mind that it was the right day to meet with my best friend, death. It was in the evening around 9 p.m. that I decided to take my life. My nephew Kogi, cousin Ben, and Maina, our roommate, were at a nearby pub drinking beer. I went to get the house key from them, and then I went back home, opened the house, and sat down on the bed to think. After a couple of minutes, I poured some water into a glass, ready to overdose on Malaria-Quinn tablets, but I had to pray first.

This was my prayer:

God, your son Charles Elephant is on his way home; please send your angels to welcome and lead me home. I cannot blame you for my death. Lord, you have given me life to live and I am grateful for that. It's I who does not want to live in this merciless and bitter world. My prayer has been to bless me with death. But Lord, giving me life is to give me a stone instead of bread. I am dying to receive this bread because I have been hungry for so long, and now my hunger is coming to an end. But Lord, I have to apologize to you first because you had a purpose for me, and now it will not be done. I am sorry about this premature death, but for now it is the best bread I can have. I wanted to write a book for people to read and draw them closer to you, but all those were my daydreams. But God, let everything be done according to your will...

I continued with my prayers and fell asleep while the oil lamp was still on. When my nephew came back home with my cousin, they knocked on the door for me to open up. I was shocked to find the tablets and water still on the table. They were drunk and therefore could not understand anything. They asked me whether I was ill, and I told them that I felt like I was suffering from Malaria.

The next evening I did the same thing, and it happened the same way. The second time I knew it was not the will of God for me to die, and therefore I could not try the third time.

On the third day, God sent a lady called Hannah with a message for me. To my surprise, it was my first time meeting her, but she knew what I was going through. In fact, all along I thought it was a secret between God and me. She said to me, "Charles, God loves you so much, and he is not ready to give you what you are praying for. God's will is to give you anything else except death. He has good plans for you, if only you give Him a chance." I replied to her, "Go back and tell God that I have appreciated His concern, but I am sorry. I need nothing else in this world except death."

She tried to persuade me to withdraw my request, but it was all in vain. At this point, I said to her, "Hannah, you were sent to give me a message, but not to discuss it with me. Please do honor my reply, too. Go and tell Him that Charles wants to die."

The second time, God sent her with the same message. I replied the same way without remorse.

The third time, I had softened my heart, but at first I was stubborn, as usual, though I was willing to listen to her. In fact, I do not argue with God after the second time. I am always ready to compromise the third time. She took the time to explain to me about the love of God and the purpose He had for me. After she was done explaining, I asked her why God was not willing to give me what I really needed at that time. She could not tell me the reason, but since I had made up my mind not to fight against God's will the third time, then I had to give in. I sent her back with a message that I had accepted His will, but that I needed a Master's degree.

The next day, God sent Hannah with a message that He had blessed me with the sort of education that I may desire in this world. To me, receiving a Master's degree was the hardest and most impossible goal I could set in my life, since I was a fourth form dropout. Also, I could not trust my mind because I was depressed, and the glue that I had sniffed had affected my mind. To be truthful, I could open a page to read it, but if I closed the page, I could no longer tell you what I had been reading. I knew the first work God had to do was to renew my mind. Those factors to me made it impossible to go back to school, but God is awesome, and he made everything possible.

In the evening, I made my vows with God, and this was my prayer:

God, my life had come to an end, but you have persuaded me to live. I believe that you love me and have a good purpose for me. From now on, I have surrendered my life to you. Each minute I live henceforth is no longer mine but yours. I will no longer live my own life but yours. All that I want in this world is to make you happy by doing according to your will. Please take me, Lord, and make me righteous and holy again. Lord, I believe your word is final because no one is above you. Lord, if you declare me righteous and holy, I will be holy in deed and no one can accuse you. I want you, Lord, to live in me, and the Charles in me should die. Lord, I declare to you that my life is over and yours has just begun. I do not want to live like human beings; I want to live like you. Let my body be your dwelling place to administer to the world. Let the world receive your blessings through me. Let the purest river of crystal that flows from you and the lamb join and pass through me in order to feed your children with the water of life. Let the tree of life that bears twelve types of fruits, twelve times a year, grow within me in order to feed your children. Let your tree of healing grow in me so that I can heal the nations, tribes, and races. Let the tree of love grow in me so that I can love you and your children, too.

From today, the world may have no place for you to stay, but my body I confidently offer to you as a shelter. Make sure Charles does not rise again, but let Jesus arise in me. Father, if you feel that I am not doing your will, or that I am worthless, please do not hesitate to take my life away instead of leaving me in this world alone. Take my soul and hide it in your soul, where my enemies cannot reach me. I do not want to live any longer, but I want you to live in me in order to shine out into the world.

Lord, do not forget that I am your precious infant, and in case you leave me alone, you will find me dead. Please take good care of your infant, Charles, and you will be proud of me. I commit my soul, my body, and my mind to you, alone. I have nothing better to offer to you because I am poor and have nothing except myself. Lord, do not reject my offering and sacrifices that I bring to your Holy altar. Lord, I want you to teach me your will in a simple way that I can understand, and I will teach the rest of the world. In this regard, I do not want to read of your great deeds; I want to receive those miracles and also to repeat in my dreams and visions exactly what happened in ancient times. Let the Bible be my reference, but I want you to be my teacher. I do not want to read that you used to talk to Moses and other prophets; I want you to talk to me. I do not want you to send people to me; I want you to communicate directly to me because you are in me and you are my Father and above all my best friend. I want you to teach me because I am your child.

God, I believe you did not call me to have a big title in this world; the only title I want is to be called "the loved child." You can use me to bless your children in any way so long as you do not give me those big titles because I am content with being your child. God, I am ready to be your child and your best friend. Amen.

I slept, but the problems did not come to an end. In fact, it was only the beginning. After that, I began beseeching God with all my heart. I taught myself how to listen to His voice.

In December 1988, I decided to develop a career in computer studies. I went to one college and got information regarding the courses. The next weekend, I decided to go home on a Sunday to inform my father in upcountry so that he could pay for me or request that my sisters or brother do so. I informed God about my intention and He blessed my ideas.

One Sunday, I woke up very early in the morning. I passed by my brother's house, to inform him about my journey, but he could not understand why I had decided at once to go home. He tried to convince me not to go and instead to wait until Christmas, but there was a force that was driving me crazy. Actually, I could hear a voice telling me, "Charles, leave your brother alone. He cannot understand what you are saying. You do not need his permission." I left him and proceeded on my journey home.

I arrived home around 11 a.m. I found my parents and my twin sister. I told my parents my plan, and they were very happy with the idea that I might go back to school. My dad promised me that everything would be fine, and he would talk to the rest of the family to see how they could support me. During the Christmas holiday, God warned me in a dream not to go home. He also told me that there was no hope of being assisted, but He assured me not to worry because he would provide me with school fees if only I trusted in Him.

My brother and some of my sisters went home for the Christmas holiday. I understood that my dad mentioned the idea to my brother, who strongly opposed the idea. My brother convinced my dad that a computer course was not good and that I was a liar. All that I wanted was money to go to movies and discos, and I did not deserve to be supported. My dad was convinced that I was a liar and that my intention was to con him. That made him angry with me.

I went home on New Year's Eve, 1988. I arrived home around midday, though I was not in the mood since I knew all that had happened, but I was strong in God. I met everybody at home, and no one seemed excited to see me. I greeted them all except my dad, who refused to greet me. After that, I went to sleep in the granary (where dry maize or corns are stored because it used to be my place to sleep). By coincidence, my brother and my elder sister came and sat near the granary because the sun was hot. My brother started boasting about how I would not go to school because I was lazy and selfish, among other things.

After they left, I got up and went to visit my friends just to be away from home. I spent one week with my friends, and only returned to my home during the day. My twin sister sympathized with me, but I told her not to worry about me because on the 7th of January, 1989, I would be in school with or without money because my God is alive. I confessed to her that my God would provide, and I should not worry because He cares for me just the same way He provided Abraham with a lamb on the mountain when Abraham wanted to sacrifice his son, Isaac. Parents, relatives, and friends might forsake me in times of need, but God would never forsake me. Those who truly trust God will never fail in their plans or lack anything, though the whole world might be against them.

My twin sister could not understand what I was telling her, and I promised her that when I went back to Nairobi, I would not come back home until the day God blessed me with a job, no matter what happened at home.

When the holidays were over, I went back to Nairobi without having a single word with my dad. I had resigned from the shoe making company (C&P) where I was working in December 1988 as a step of faith and trusted in God for everything. I took a step forward, certain that I would be in college in January. My brother-in-law became concerned and decided to give me the fee for college for two months while sorting out my case. So, on the 7th of January, at 2 p.m., I was seated in a computer class with other students, waiting for the teacher to come. My brother had earlier told me that as soon as I entered the classroom, then I should leave his house. In other words, not to go back to his place, but I knew my God was faithful and would not let me down.

Since then, God has sponsored me in several courses in various fields, and today I have attained two Master's Degrees. At present, I am pursuing a third one from a university in the United States. God has kept His precious promise that He made with me. I asked for one Master's Degree, but He blessed me with plenty, and I am looking forward to a doctorate. The sky is the limit in acquiring knowledge. He blessed me with any education I might desire in this world, Glory be to God on high. The impossibilities were turned into possibilities.

I do not know if God is calling you today, but what I do know is that God has a good purpose for each of us. We cannot know God's purpose until we answer unto His call. Sometime we waste time or get confused because there is a supernatural power that drives us or leads our lives when we fight His calling.

If you find that you cannot understand why and how things are happening in your life or you cannot find your own identity, then God is calling you. Stop making your life miserable by trying to fight or wrestle with God. Simply answer unto His call. God, your child, your servant is listening. I am ready to do your will. Send me and I will go, use me and I will glorify your name. Take my soul and mind because there are no longer my own. God, the Creator of the universe, let your will be done in my life for your glory. Do not harden your heart.

CHAPTER 6

SUBMITTING MY LIFE TO GOD

This chapter explains how I answered God's call. One of the reasons why I decided to analyze my life in detail is to set example to others who might be going through the same process that I did. It is hard to recognize God's voice, especially in the midst of suffering, because His voice is soft and gentle. There was no one to explain this to me and therefore, at first, I thought I was crazy. This book will help many to reflect on their lives and to be able to answer God's call at the right time and at the right place. God does not use force or commands; He uses Love. He does not exercise His power but His authority. He gave us total freedom and therefore He does respect our decisions. He does not intimidate or threaten us to follow Him because God is not desperate, but He is calling with love. At first I could not understand the meaning of love and salvation, nor did I understand the role of Jesus in heaven.

After receiving the miracle of going to school, I believed that God knew me by my name. I made a promise to myself that I must hold on to the opportunity God had granted me to know Him. I knew it would take time to do so, but to me that did not matter because I had nothing to lose. I opened my heart to receive from Him so that I could teach the world about His grace, mercy, favor and love. I felt obliged to give back to the world something in some small way. I therefore decided to live a heavenly life, to be a part of the fellowship in heaven. My assumption was that no one else existed in this world that I could turn to or lean on except God. I set my mind and soul to focus on God as my helper and my best friend. I chose to listen to God's teachings and corrections in order to tap into wisdom directly from Him. It did not matter what the world said or agreed upon. I cared about God's will. I desired to be God's advocate, to tell people what God required from them, instead of being the people's advocate, to tell God what people required. Church leaders are the voice of the people to God, while prophets are the voice of God to people. Therefore, I chose to be the voice of God to people.

As soon as I joined college, God started revealing Himself to me in a mighty way. Sometimes He could do so in dreams or visions or by speaking as a soft voice in my ears. I learned how to recognize His voice and how to interpret his dreams and visions. It has taken me years, but it has been worth it. At the same time, God would give me messages to deliver to people and or send me to pray for the sick in the hospital as a part of his teachings. It was amazing, because at that time, I did not know who Jesus was to me. Those to whom I was sent were born-again Christians, and they expected me to share testimony with them, but I could only deliver the message. After delivering the message, some would give me their testimonies and then ask me to give mine. I would respond with this: "The salvation is between me and God. I came to deliver your message but not to discuss my relationship with God." They would wonder why God was using me, and hence many doubted me.

One time, I was sent to a certain lady who was holding a big position in one of the powerful churches in Kenya. I went with another lady, with whom we held fellowship. A visitor who came later with her husband was given the red-carpet treatment while we were made to wait for more than two hours. The others sat at a dining table to eat and to drink because it was lunchtime, but we were only given tea and were not allowed to sit together at the same table. We had to be patient because the message had to be delivered, and we had not gone there just to eat.

When the visitor left, then we were given attention. I delivered the message that I had for her but she doubted. She could not understand why God could not use people in her church, and she wondered also why I was being used even though, in her mind, I was not saved. Yet the message I gave to her was true. I went home disturbed because I thought that perhaps God had not sent me, after all.

That night, as I was half-asleep, I saw myself kneeling down, crying and praying to intercede for a lady because she was in darkness while I was surrounded by a beautiful, bright light. Then I identified the lady as the same lady to whom I had delivered the message. I heard a voice in my dream telling me not to worry; she doubted because she was in darkness, though holding a high position in the church. God does not associate us with churches but He knows us by our names.

I woke up the following day relieved. Since then, anytime I deliver a message to anyone, whether a person accepts it or not, it does not bother me.

In November 1989, I got a temporary job with a petroleum company for about six months. In December of the same year, my grandmother died, and I went home to attend the funeral. I decided to attend the funeral without spending the night at home. I arrived at home in the morning, and I was well received. After the funeral, my dad escorted me to the bus terminus. While on the way, I gave him Kshs.50 note to buy cigarettes. He could not believe his eyes; he took it, looked at it, and shed tears after recalling how he had mistreated me all those years before. I took a bus back to Nairobi.

Not Understanding Salvation

I had no understanding of the meaning of salvation and the role of Jesus Christ in my life. Since I had made up my mind to follow God and not to pay attention to human beings, I had to pray for revelation to know who Jesus was. The question that was puzzling me most was this: Who is greater of these three? If God granted His kingdom to Jesus, where then did He go, because He had to leave anyway? According to the Bible, He said that He is the only God to be worshipped; so why then do we refer to Jesus as God? I did not know whether to pray to God or to Jesus because I could not understand their roles. I could not understand why we rebuke the Devil and cast out the demons in the name of Jesus but not in the name of Jehovah God. To me, if Jesus was greater, it meant that God had left to go to another kingdom because He could not have demoted Himself. The other issue was that when God called me, He identified himself as Jehovah God, the Creator of the universe and its inheritance, the only God to be worshipped. Then who was Jesus and why do we worship him?

Therefore, this was my prayer:

My heavenly Father, I believe you love and care for me. I believe that you did not call me to be puzzled by your ways but to make your ways clear, simple, and well known to me. I believe you called me to teach me in a simple and not complicated way nor to confuse me in that matter. Therefore, please Lord; answer me in a simple and concise way. Who is greater between you and Jesus? What is salvation? To whom should we pray? My heavenly Father, if you want me to confess that I am saved, I would request you to come down from heaven and tell me to do so, but please do not send anyone, including angels, because I will not listen to them. I want to hear from you and you alone, just the same way you called me without sending anyone; even now I need to hear from you alone. Amen.

Acknowledging Jesus

One night thereafter, I went to sleep as usual. Within a short time, I felt only half-asleep, and I saw a vision. At first, I started feeling a lot of heat, as if there was a heating system in the room that made me sweat, and I became uncomfortable. But I was paralyzed on one side, so that I could not turn. I saw the roof of the house open and a stepladder started descending from heaven to where I was lying on my bed. I saw someone, wearing a red velvet robe, climbing down the stepladder, holding a huge, black book. The stepladder became a chair, and he sat on it facing me while I was still lying on the bed. He said, "Charles, I am Jehovah God, your Father, the Creator of the universe, and I have done according to your will, and now it is your turn to do my will. You have made me come down from heaven, and in this case, if you do not acknowledge Jesus as your personal savior and confess to people, I will kill you."

He did not talk much, but by the time he left, I had said, "Jesus is the Lord" a thousand times. When he left, I woke up and found that I was still sweating; my bedding was all wet. I had to open the door because the room was still hot. The next morning, I changed my greetings and started praising Jesus Christ as my savior.

Explanation

Later, in another dream, God explained the role of Jesus Christ. God is the creator of the universe and its inheritance. Therefore, He is the Father of all creation. He is a living God who changes not. There is no other God except Him and His name is Jehovah God. He does not share His glory with anyone either in heaven or on earth.

God blessed the world through Jesus the Christ to teach people about His will and also to be sacrificed in order to cleanse us from the original sins or curses. Jesus came to save mankind from the wrath of God. Jesus did not come to overthrow or replace his God but to connect mankind with God. He brought understanding between mankind and God to seal the gap that was created as a result of sins between man and God. He never called himself God, but instead the son of a man or the living God. He accepted God's offer to be the king in the house of the Lord and therefore, he was ready for the consequences.

After accomplishing the work that God had given him, God crowned and made him a king in his kingdom. He is the favorite king to rule in the house of Jehovah God. He was given the universe to rule, though God Jehovah remains the supreme king and the God of the entire creation. God created man and made him the ruler of the world, but man foolishly gave his rights away to the Devil. Therefore, God could no longer trust man and that is why He chose Jesus to be a king to rule over mankind. Jesus taught people about God his Father, who is also our Father. He taught his disciples how to pray to our heavenly Father, not to him. Jesus himself was a great prayer warrior. He never waited for things to happen because he was the Son of God, but he could proceed to the mountain alone to pray, especially during the night. The prayers were to keep him in touch or connected with his Father, to understand his mission and to know whether he was doing the right thing.

Prayer is an effective communication between God and man. Through prayers, man is able to understand God's will and to gain God's favor. Before the hour came for Jesus to suffer, he painfully prayed on the mountain for his will to be done by asking God to take away the cup of suffering. But he remembered that it was not his will that he had come to do in this world, but God's will. He quickly withdrew his request and allowed for the will of God to be done. He taught us how to honor and respect God as the creator of the universe and above all, as a loving and caring Father.

Jesus is the beginning and the end of everything. He is the beginning in the sense that he was the first one to be created by God. He is the end because he will judge the world and its inheritance on the last day of this world. Everything will come to an end, but God's kingdom will last forever. God gave him the power and authority to judge and to rule the world forever. He is the Alpha and Omega.

God has two gifts to give because there are two kingdoms that exist. On his left hand is the kingdom of darkness (the evil) with Lucifer (Devil) as the king. On the right hand is the kingdom of righteousness (the good) with Jesus as the king. Lucifer does not fight God himself, but he fights Jesus. The war is because they compete for mankind. God gave Jesus the keys of heaven and hell, and also the authority and power, but the Devil refuses to recognize Jesus as a king in the house of God. Jesus came to destroy the work of the Devil, and the Devil destroys the work of Jesus, too. That is why we rebuke or cast out the power of darkness or evil spirits and demons in the name of Jesus the Christ but not Jehovah God. The name Jesus has the power and authority above all the names in the Universe except Jehovah God. Prayer requests are made to God our Father through Jesus Christ. God is the provider of everything and therefore addressing Him through Jesus means that Jesus will intercede on our behalf.

Jesus is the advocate of all those who sincerely acknowledge and honor his suffering. He does not condemn anyone but prays for every soul to be saved. Jesus is a king of kings but not God, because there is only one God in the universe. There should be no other God except Jehovah God. Christians have broken the first and second commandments that warn mankind not to hold or create any other god in heaven or on earth. The people decided to declare Jesus as God but to Jehovah God, Jesus is a king of kings in His house. The reason why Jesus is a king of kings is because in the house of God, there will be many kings who will reign with Jesus, but Jesus will be the king overall.

But man always changes the will of God to suit himself. God promised an everlasting king in the reign of David, but He did not promise a god. If anyone wants to argue it, we are all in the likeness of God and therefore we are all gods, the sons of the Most High God (Psalm 82:6). Jehovah God introduced Jesus to the world as his son, not as a god or his partner. According to Matthew 3:16-17, *as soon as Jesus was baptized, he came up out of the water. Then heaven was opened to him, and he saw the Spirit of God coming down like a dove alighting upon him. Then a voice said from heaven, "This is my own dear Son, with whom I am pleased."*

God gave Jesus many titles, such as the "Wonderful Councilor," because he was full of wonders and miracles. "Emmanuel" means God to us because he came to be the light of the world and to bring God's presence to mankind. Jesus is called the "Messiah," because according to the prophet Isaiah, Jesus was the anointed one to bring salvation to mankind. He is the savior.

This has not been clear to many Christians. Jesus said that there is only one who is Holy and worthy of being worshipped and praised. He acknowledged the fact that the suffering was not his will but the will of his Father. He also said that only God knows seasons and time, no one else, including the angels. In fact, God revealed the book of *Revelation* to Jesus, then Jesus revealed it to an angel, and the angel revealed it to John, his disciple, who was put on the Island of Patmos because he proclaimed the word of God.

By the way, the book of the *Revelation* is the most powerful book in the Bible because it has the prophetic words of the things to come. Therefore, the churches must teach about it most instead of only history.

Receiving Baptism from the Holy Ghost

Some few days after God had descended from heaven to tell me to be saved, the Holy Spirit of God took control of me. Then I was led into a lake of fire. I found someone who was waiting for me. I recognized him because he was wearing the same red velvet robe he had been wearing when He descended from heaven to tell me to be saved. He got hold of my hand and threw me into the lake of fire. The fire was too hot, and I tried to run away by swimming, but He walked upon the fire, pushing me back into the deep part. He said, "Charles, I am God your Father. I have come to baptize you with the fire of the Holy Ghost so that you can be holy like us."

He turned me around seven times. By then I was seriously burned, and due to the pain, I was able to speak in several languages (tongues) that I could not understand. Later, He took me out of the fire and told me to go and proclaim that the day of the Lord is at hand. I went back and woke up. My bed sheets were completely wet, and my body was, too. I have never felt such heat in my life.

A few weeks later, while I was sleeping during the day, I saw heaven open and someone with a light cream robe descended, holding a bottle of oil. He said to me, "Charles, I am Jesus, who died for your sins. I have been sent by God our Father to anoint you because God has chosen you from the world." He opened the bottle and poured the whole bottle on me. The oil came down over my head onto the T-shirt that I was wearing. What surprised me was its fragrance. It was cool and refreshed me. Then Jesus left.

It is good to believe in things that we cannot see or touch or hear, unlike Thomas who doubted and only believed because he touched the scars of the nails on Jesus body. Yet, on the other hand, it is also better to seek for the truth from God. In fact, Thomas was the only man who was blessed or allowed to touch Jesus after his resurrection.

CHAPTER 7

EXCITING MISSIONS

Now after this occasion, I became well aware of my destiny and I was ready to perform God's will. God teaches us about his love and will, for we are his children. He does not expect us to do things that we are not aware of. He understands our strengths and weaknesses. He does not force us to do His will but plans and creates a need for us to do His will. In this chapter I describe two missions. The first one I hesitated to go on, but the second one I was more than willing to do.

A Sick Person

In 1990, one day I was sent to the hospital to cleanse a sick person, whom God wanted to take home. I was given all the details to identify him. But I refused to go because at that time I was affected psychologically after visiting patients in the hospital. God spoke to me and said he would not look for someone else to cleanse the man because it was for me to do, but I refused to go.

A week later, on a Saturday afternoon, I had agreed to meet with my classmate for a class work assignment discussion. I went to her place and found her waiting for me, but she was blue and looked dull. I said hello to her, and then I asked her what was wrong. She started sobbing while telling me about her brother-in-law, who had been admitted to the hospital. She said we could not have our class discussion, but she did ask that I accompany her to the hospital because the rest of her family had already gone. At this juncture I could not say no because I had no other plans for the day, and surprisingly, I had forgotten about my hospital issue.

It was around 5:30 p.m. We took a bus to the hospital. As we were going, she told me that her brother-in-law had been sick for more than a week. We arrived at the hospital at around 6:30 p.m., and visiting hours were over. We pleaded with the nurse to allow us in for five minutes only. She allowed us to go in, but what shocked me was the setting of the ward. The curtains and bedding were exactly the same description I had been given. I came back to my senses and recalled the message I was meant to deliver. I placed my hand on him and prayed silently, *"God, I have done your will, please let it be done according to your will. I commit this man unto your hands to cleanse him and forgive his sins. Amen."*

We left the ward and took the elevator down without talking to each other because I did not know how to explain anything to her, though I knew it was done. As we were still inside the elevator, I heard a soft voice that said to me, *"Charles, you cannot compete with me because my ways are not your ways. Comfort the family because their brother is going to die tonight."* I was given a scripture from the holy Bible (1 Thessalonians 3:13-18) for the family to read after arriving home. We found the other family members waiting outside, and I told them about the love of God and how He is still in the business of blessing and caring for us. Then I gave them the scripture, and I went on my way home at around 7 p.m.

The next day, at around 10 a.m., my friend (the one I had accompanied to the hospital) called and said to me, "Charles, I would like to express my gratitude on behalf of the entire family for your comforting words. We read the verses from the Bible you gave us. It strengthened and prepared us, especially my sister. But all the same, my brother-in-law passed away yesterday. He died as soon as we left him, shortly before 7 p.m." I could barely respond to her because I was in a devastated state. I went to my room to repent and to give glory to the Lord, creator of the Universe.

One Friday night, God spoke to me and told me to go home because he had a mission for me. I did not have the bus fare, but He told me to go to the City Mortuary at 10 a.m., and I would find the means of transportation waiting for me. He told me not to worry about coming back because the return fare had been given to my mom, and I should go back to Nairobi on Tuesday.

I woke up early in the morning and did as I had been told. To my surprise, I met people whom I knew from home who had come to collect the remains of a family member. There was a lorry (truck) provided by her workplace, and it was empty. As I was standing alone somewhere, Nelson, who was a family member to the deceased, and a neighbor approached and asked me if I was interested in joining them. They said that I could board the truck that was empty, though it was not in good condition. He had thought that I had gone to view the body. I agreed, and soon the procession started heading for home.

We arrived home in the afternoon, and the funeral services started at around 4 p.m. Later in the evening, after the funeral was over, my friend Nelson and I walked home. I thought that the mission had been about attending the funeral, since God had not told me anything else regarding the mission.

As we were walking home, we met a neighboring lady, Mama Njeri, who was coming from a local church. She told us about their pastor, who had been admitted to a certain local hospital, and I did not bother much because I did not know him in the first place. My friend Nelson kept the conversation going by asking her questions. We arrived at a junction and parted ways with her. We first went to my place with Nelson and later to his place to spend the night there.

At night, I was half-asleep when at once the room was filled with a beautiful and glorious bright light. The spirit of God took control of me and took me to the hospital where the pastor was lying on a bed. I was shown the bed, given his name, and was able to identify him. The message was to tell him to cleanse himself because God wanted to bless him; God had revealed to me that He wanted to take him home, though I could not tell him that. God instructed me to request that the lady whom we had met go with me. Regarding the bus fare, God told me that He had blessed her with the money, since I had nothing in my pocket, and it was quite a distance.

The next day, I was totally confused because in the first place, this Mama Njeri did not know that I was saved or that God used me. She only knew me from the time I was young, as a worshipper. Actually, she used to preach to me to be saved, but I never gave in.

Later in the day, I went to her place and told her about the message that I had regarding her pastor. She was amazed because she could not imagine that I had won God's favor. I requested her to deliver the message because I did not have bus fare, but she refused. She looked at me and said, "Charles, I am proud of you, and I am willing to go with you, but I have no money for both of us." I asked her how much money she had, and she said that she had fare for one person to and from the hospital. To me it was more than enough. I asked her, "So you mean you have fare for two people to go?" She said, "Yes." I told her, "Mama Njeri, do not worry about coming back; what is important is to be obedient and to deliver the message at the right time. If God is happy with us, He will provide the means to come back home. We do not have to beg because He is a loving and caring Father. All the same, we can walk home even if it would take us two or three hours; God will refresh our strength and make our journey shorter."

We agreed to go the next day at lunchtime because that was the time God had instructed me to be at the gate.

On Monday, we met at 10 a.m. The sky was blue, and we took off to the bus terminal. We took a Matatu to Tumutumu Mission Hospital. We alighted the vehicle some minutes past midday. We walked for about a half an hour and arrived at the hospital a few minutes before 1 p.m. I warned Mama Njeri never to mention that we did not have bus fare, because I did not want us to be a burden or to shame the name of the living God.

We waited patiently at the main gate for the gate to be opened for visitors. At 1 p.m., the main gate was opened, and we walked in towards the ward where the pastor was admitted. We went straight to the bed; Mama Njeri introduced me to him and left us to talk. As soon as she left the room, it started to rain outside without warning, which kept the pastor's wife, friends, and relatives at a distance on another block for about fifteen minutes. I delivered the message to him and we prayed together without interference. As soon as we were through, the rain stopped, and his visitors came in. The pastor introduced me to his wife and friends. After a little while, I requested permission to leave because we had to get ready to walk back, and I did not want others to notice that we did not have bus fare, after serving the living God.

A pastor from the same church, but in another parish, requested me to lead them in prayer and thereafter we bid them a word of farewell, though he did not know me. After the prayers, we left the room and Mama Njeri was astonished, but she could not say a word.

We started walking home since we had no money in our pockets, but we had the joy of the Lord because we had done according to His will. I started telling her about my encounter with God and the love that God has for mankind. After walking for quite a distance, we were near the Tana River Bridge (Gatiki) on our way home. A car from the Kenya Power & Lighting Company approached. Immediately upon reaching where we were, the driver stopped the car. He greeted us and then asked whether we could help them by giving them directions because they were lost. They were from Nyeri town, and they had received an emergency call from a certain high school. I interrupted him by asking him where they were intending to go. He replied, "We are going to Kiangoma High School in Mukurwe-ini division." I laughed because I knew it was a miracle. They had passed the school and driven about fifteen kilometers out of their way, and in fact, the school was our neighbor. It was where I had gone for primary education.

I told the driver that we were willing to help them if only they could give us a lift. He told us to board the car, made a U-turn, and drove back. We were dropped near home, and they proceeded to Kiangoma High School. By that time, Mama Njeri was in total shock and was left speechless.

After alighting, I looked at her, smiled, and said, "Oh, what a loving and caring God we have served." She could not comment about it. I went back home and asked my mom to give me fare to go back to Nairobi the next day. She told me that she did not have money, but that very day someone who owed her some money had paid her back— Kshs 200. It was the exact amount I needed for the bus fare back to Nairobi.

That night, in a vision, I saw that the Devil was not happy with me. I saw him pulling two passenger cars from different directions and causing them to collide head on because he thought that I was in one of them, and some passengers died. After praying about it, God instructed me regarding what time to board a Nissan Matatu. He further told me that there would be three Nissans Matatus waiting in a queue. The first one would be almost full, the second would have only a few passengers, and the third one would be completely empty. He told me that we should board the third one. I was still with my neighbor, Nelson; we followed His instructions, though I did not tell Nelson the reason. As soon as the Nissan was full, it took off and we were on our way to Nairobi. Later, we found out that an accident had occurred about half an hour earlier, before we arrived at the scene, and that two or three people had been killed on the spot. They were still lying there, waiting to be collected by the police. Two Nissan Matatus from opposite directions had been involved in a head-on collision.

Later, Mama Njeri testified to the members of her congregation, including the wife of the pastor, regarding all that had happened. After two weeks, the pastor passed away, and there was worshipping and praising because God had prepared and blessed them with peace and joy.

The next day, after I returned to Nairobi, God instructed me to go to Ngong Hill for overnight prayers. Ngong Hill is a game park that has wild animals. I feared to go because of the wild animals, but I told God to confirm to me that the wild animals would do me no harm. That night I saw a vision where all the wild animals were surrounding me and were very friendly, including the lions. After this wonderful confirmation, I became very brave, and I was looking forward to the next day.

The next day, I went to Ngong Hill for an overnight prayer, and since then I have been going there now and then to praise and worship the God of the universe. Today I do not fear anything because I know God can tame any wild animal.

God is simple and His ways are simple too. He does not move the mountain for us to know that He is God but He teaches us with simple examples that we can understand and appreciate because they are apart of our own lives. His examples always consist of things or events or people that we know, to make it easier for us. God also treats us with love and kindness. He leads us without condemnation. When we go astray or fail to do His will due to our ignorance, He corrects us with love. His love to us endures forever.

CHAPTER 8

THE OCCASION OF MY BIRTHDAY

God is a caring and loving Father. I did not know that God is concerned about our lives and ready to make us happy or give us surprises. I invited God for my birthday and He responded positively. God is awesome.

Birthday Gifts

It was 1993 and the occasion of my birthday, and I thought it was a good idea to invite God, since I had not received a birthday card in my whole life. Some few days before my birthday, I made my request known to Him. The eve of my birthday, as I was sleeping, Jesus appeared to me in a dream, and he was holding a key. He took me to a building with twelve rooms, six on the ground floor and six upstairs. While holding the key, he said to me, "Charles, I have been sent to you by God to bring this key as a birthday gift to you." He opened the main door and then took me around the rooms. The walls and floors were painted white. I asked him, "Jesus, what does God say about me?" I asked because I thought perhaps God did not like me due to my stubbornness. He said to me, "Charles, God loves you very much." He handed the key to me and left.

The heavenly Father sent me a different kind of birthday gift. It was on the eve of my birthday, and again I was half-asleep when the heavens opened. I saw a scroll coming down. When it reached about ten meters above the ground, it stopped and floated in the air. Upon it was written, "Charles, my love is for you." It had a rose in the middle, which changed colors. This birthday card was so beautiful, and the glory that had covered it was beyond my imagination or explanation. After some time, it was rolled up.

On the third birthday after that, my heavenly Father sent me a bouquet of orange and red roses. An angel appeared to me holding orange roses in a dream and told me that it was a birthday gift. It was the first time I had ever seen an orange rose; it had not occurred to me that there were orange-red flowers. Actually, I had forgotten that it was my birthday. The angel told me to receive it as a symbol of love from God. Then he opened a room for me and told me to enter. The floor was covered with red and orange roses, forming a bed. I was so happy, I started jumping and rolling myself on the bed of roses. I was dancing and shouting with joy. I enjoyed that room for several hours.

God is ready to bless us according to our heart's desires. Surely, as Jesus said in his teachings, no man who can be asked by his child for bread can give only a stone, or asked for a fish, give only a snake. In the same way, our heavenly Father can do much more than an earthly father. We only need to be faithful to him and He will bless us according to the riches of heaven.

CHAPTER 9

LOVE

Love is the greatest gift of all because we cannot define or explain it. It is in the name of love that we sacrifice our lives. Jesus sacrificed his life for our sake because of the Love God had for the world. Love can only be taught practically, because in most cases that is the only way we can understand its power. Without love, there could be no world. God made me to go through the practical experience of being hurt, disappointed, desperate and discouraged. Without suffering, love could have no value; suffering draws us closer to God and helps us to appreciate the gift of life. This, I know.

Lesson of Love

In 1990, I asked God to teach me about love because I could not understand the meaning of the word love and why God is love. Also, I could not understand why God is so concerned with human beings despite our sins, which we commit every day. God always talks about love, and that is why I wanted to know and understand the true meaning from Him.

The first thing he taught me was about the spiritual journey. In this journey, people of different kinds meet, walk together, and at some time depart in different directions. Those who walk together spiritually feel warmth for each other and attraction. They are very close and mindful of each other. Those who move away spiritually move away physically, too, and in fact they lose interest in one another. It is funny because you cannot explain it—you just feel bored by one another or you feel a lack of closeness.

One day, God told me to pray for a helper, and I did. One evening I went to Ngong for overnight prayers together with a group of worshippers, whom I had met a few days ago. At Ngong, I met several new people, whom I had not met before. In that group, I was the only one who could not speak in tongues, and therefore the team prayer worrier decided to pray for me to be filled with new tongues.

In the evening at around 8 p.m., I was told to kneel down and lift up my hands to pray, and everybody else was praying for me, too. I prayed for about an hour, but nothing happened. They told me to shout Halleluiah without stopping, and that took me about another hour. I became exhausted, almost to the point of collapse, yet nothing happened. They assumed that I was a sinner; therefore, I needed to repent and cleanse myself first. This made me feel like a failure, as if I was unworthy to be in the group.

The following morning we began praising and worshipping, though I was shy to lead the group in anything, since everyone believed that I was a sinner. In the evening, before the sunset, a very big dove appeared in the sky to the west. I tried to show them all, but they could not see it. This gave me courage, because as much as I could not speak in tongues, they could not see the visions. I was very foolish because I thought a vision appeared to everyone.

Later, in the evening, we decided to go and pray on our own before joining a group prayer. As soon as I was ready to start my prayers, I heard a voice asking me, "Charles, why were you shouting at me last night? Does it mean that if you ask me politely I cannot hear or satisfy your needs? Why did you leave me to go and tell other people to pray for you? Nowadays do you no longer trust me? Do you need the tongues because the others speak in tongues? You told me to communicate with you in a simple way that you could understand. That is why I refused to give you new tongues, because I do not speak in tongues to you, but now you want to be like them. Then I will give you new tongues. I will put words into your mouth, but you will never use them."

The third day, we went back home blessed in a mighty way. Since then, I do not copy or compare myself with others, and I do not shout for the Lord.

Some weeks later, I went to Ngong Hill alone, and the sun made it very hot. I sat down under a tree to read some verses from the Bible, and I heard a voice telling me to receive new tongues. I was given three words and their meanings. Truly speaking, I hardly use them; sometimes I forget that I speak in tongues. This lesson taught me not to compare myself with others because God has blessed each of us in a different way. It reminded me about the Israelites when they insisted for a physical king to be like other nations. They were given one, but it was not a blessing.

Now, among the group there was a middle-aged woman called Mama Kihanya, who was very humble and never used to talk a lot. During prayers, she requested us to pray for her daughter, Mary, who was not saved. To me, it was none of my concern, because I did not know the family in the first place. On Sunday morning, we went back home after spending three days at Ngong Hill praying.

One day, I was sent to take a message to Mama Kihanya at her home. I went there and met her with her friend Margaret. When my time came to leave, they escorted me to a bus stop. I boarded the bus, and they left before the bus pulled away. As they were walking away, I heard a voice asking me, "Charles, what would you think if Mama Kihanya became your mother-in-love?" At first, I gave a jeering laugh, and then replied that I did not have any problem with that. It had not occurred to me that she had a grown-up daughter, and I thought that the one for whom we were praying was a kid who was refusing to go to school.

Another time in a dream, God asked me, "Charles, how would you react if I give you a girl who is not saved nor a committed Christian?" I knew that this was a test, and I said, "Lord, what you have made holy is holy in deed. Your choice is my choice because I know your choice is always the best. The salvation comes from you, God, and in fact it is the relationship between you and her. All that I need is love, respect, and obedience from her. It was through your grace and favor that I was saved; otherwise, I was no better than her." He told me that she might or might not be the one, and therefore I should not take her as my wife.

One afternoon, the whole group was to meet in someone's house for prayers. Mama Kihanya was there, together with other acquaintances. I went there and found that the whole group was there for prayers. Mama Kihanya was quite disturbed because she could not understand why God was willing to give me her unsaved girl. God had already revealed this to her through another lady, who had been sent to her. She told her friend Margaret, who was courageous enough to break the news to me in order to see my reaction.

After prayers, we started departing in different directions. As I was saying goodbye, Margaret asked me to escort her. I said yes and immediately she stood up. We started walking towards the bus stop, but she was "beating about the bush," and I could read her mind regarding what she wanted to tell me. I encouraged her to tell me in straightforward terms what she wanted to tell me. At that time, she told me how Mama Kihanya was worried regarding the message she had gotten. I asked her to be specific, and she told me that God had talked about my relationship with Mama Kihanya's daughter. Her worry was whether I would take her daughter or not. I told her to go back and tell her friend Mama Kihanya not to worry. What God has made holy is holy in deed. With or without her daughter, I accepted her as my mother-in-love. I am a child of God, and her daughter is a child of God, too. Therefore, God has a right to do whatever pleases Him. No man could save or make himself holy or righteous except God.

She was happy and went back to tell Mama Kihanya about my response. At that time, I had not met her daughter.

One night in a dream, I was told to visit Mama Kihanya's place. I went there the next morning, and I met the daughter for the first time. I was not comfortable with her because she was very beautiful, and that made me think that I did not deserve her. As soon as I left their place, I said no to God. I tried to give all the reasons to justify my argument, but they were all in vain. I decided to keep my distance, but to obey because I knew it was a tough lesson. We did not communicate, though sometimes I would meet her accidentally at her home.

As time went by, I came to love her because I did not have an option. God told me in a dream that He loved me before I knew Him and hence taught me how to love Him, since at first I did not have love for

Him. So, it was the same way, I had to love someone who did not love me, and to teach her how to love me. I decided to accept her in my heart, and I could send gifts and greetings cards occasionally, including a Bible, though God never allowed me to have good times with her. It was all contrary to what I had imagined—I thought it would be an easy road, but it turned out to be tough.

I remember one day, a certain company wanted someone to work for one month. She had qualified for the position. I thought it was a good idea to inform her about it. I called her but received no response, so I decided to go to their place because she was supposed to report the next day. I went there and knocked on the door, and her cousin Sylvia greeted me. I asked about her cousin, Mary. Sylvia told me that she did not know where her cousin was. I left the message with her to tell her cousin to call me as soon as possible about an urgent matter. I felt so bad because I knew she was lying to me; in fact, as she was talking to me, another voice confirmed that it was a lie. Her cousin Mary was in the house at that time but refused to talk to me. I felt pain deep in my heart because it was my first time meeting Sylvia, and we were introduced with a lie. Mary never called me.

The next day, I went to take that job by faith. I called Mama Kihanya, who was Sylvia's aunt, and told her to warn Sylvia not to lie to me again. Sylvia was terrified because they had not told Mama Kihanya. Later, Sylvia became my best friend.

At another incident, I sent Mary a Bible as a gift, along with a Christmas card. Mary and her cousin Sylvia decided to gossip and laugh about me. This made me angry because they appeared in my vision as if they were on television, as it was happening, though I was not at their house. I later told Mama Kihanya to warn them, but this time they were horrified.

I decided never to care about her again, but God asked me in a dream, "Charles, do you want to give up on someone you love? Did I give up on you and the way you were stubborn? How will you love my people if you cannot make one person love you? How can I trust you to take care of my children?" Then I acknowledged my mistakes and apologized to him. I made the decision that I would be dedicated and make the best out of the relationship. Her life was drawn on my hand, and I could see her entire life, as the events were taking place, or about to take place, day and night. I decided to love her as a person, but not her deeds.

She had a chain of friends, though it hurt me because I knew that they were where I should have been, but I ignored it in the name of love. I could see the guys taking advantage of this poor girl, but she thought they were her friends. She would not dare listen to me, though I had a genuine and sincere love to offer to her.

One day, I called her at her place of work because I wanted to advise her to stop being reckless. She hung up the phone as soon as she recognized my voice. I felt so bad, but I remembered that it was the same way God must have felt when I was lost in sin, so I could not complain. I had thought sins were my friend, and I did not know that I was following my enemy to kill me. On the other hand, God had called me with a lot of love and care, but I never listened to Him. In fact, I used to hang up on God's calls. He pitied my wicked ways when I was lost because He could watch each and every move I was making, but I was not ready to accept His sincere love. Thank God He never gave up on me; instead, He ignored all the disappointments and discouragement I showed to him.

After a couple of years without meeting her, she appeared in my dreams wearing a cream-colored maternity dress. At that time she was pregnant. God asked me whether I had any comment regarding the issue in my dream, and He further told me that I had a choice to either accept or reject her. After two days, I approached God ready to give him my thoughts. I said, "*God, the creator of the Universe and all its inheritance, I glorify your Holy name for the love you have for me. You knew me before I knew myself. You cleansed and washed me with the precious blood of Jesus without demanding anything from me. You forgave all my sins freely and promised to love me unconditionally. Up to now, I have never been perfect the way you would like me to be, but you have never given up on me. My ways and thoughts are still wicked, but you do not grow impatient with me or condemn or punish me according to my iniquities. Even after knowing you, and you have taught me your ways, I have never lived according to your will, but instead I keep on breaking your commandments. You do not condemn me; rather you guide me on the righteous way. You teach me your ways and correct me with Love and Kindness. My heavenly Father, Mary has not wronged me or broken any of my promises because we have not made any agreements between us. In fact, if she has committed sin, then she has sinned against you, and in that case, I have no right to condemn or judge her. The door of my heart is wide open for her and the child. I am committed to loving her unconditionally, and it is the same love that has the power to heal and to forgive. If she is ready to be with me, then I have no objection. But my request to you is that you give me a chance to meet with her physically so that I can express my feelings and the love that I have for her. I will ask her in person to make a choice between me and other men. If she chooses me, I will not hesitate to take her back, but if she says no, then I will not force her. Lord, my God, I promise to respect her decision. Please help me. God, as you truly love me, help me to do the same with her. Amen.*"

God confirmed my request, but he told me that the day I would meet her, two other men would be waiting for her. God also confirmed to me that she would prefer the other men.

After a few months, she was blessed with a baby. Then after some time, one of her friends had a sick child who needed surgery, but it was very expensive. They decided to do some fundraising in order to pay the medical bill. She came to my place of work to ask that I help them by raising money with my friends, but I was not there that day. She told her mother to tell me to call her, and I was surprised, though I knew maybe God was creating a breakthrough. I called her and agreed to meet with her at 6 p.m., after work. We met, and she explained why she had wanted to see me. I agreed to help her.

After collecting all the donations, I called her and we agreed to meet so that I might give her the money. We met after work, and she bought me coffee. At 7:30 p.m., I escorted her to the bus stop. We stood there talking, and I told her about the love of God. I did not tell her more than that, as I had to wait for the day of the Lord to come.

After about a year, God instructed me in a dream to go to her mother's place. The following day was a public holiday, and I went as instructed. I met her at home with her child, her cousin Sylvia, her mom, and her dad. We had a good time, all of us, and in the evening at 7 p.m., I had to go home. Both her and her cousin decided to escort me to the bus stop. I knew that this was the day of the Lord, and I had to fulfill the promise that I had made earlier to God. I narrated to her the whole story; even quoting the events that had taken place in her private life, secretly. She was very excited and amazed about the whole story. I openly told her that I was ready to take her back as long as she was willing to be with me. I concluded by telling her that it was another day that could have marked the beginning of a new relationship. I further said to her that my door was wide open for her and her child. On the other hand, I told her about the two men waiting for her in the near future, but their relationship with her would not last for long. I told her that the men had been planted by the Devil to deceive her.

She asked me to describe the men, and I did. I gave her three weeks to think about it. Then we parted ways, and I was happy since God had made it possible, and I had fulfilled my promise, too.

After twenty-one days were over, I called her for the answer, but she said she was not ready for my offer. I could not force her to accept it, and therefore I gave glory and honor to the Lord, though deep in my heart I was mourning for her because I knew she had made the wrong choice. It did not take long before the first guy came into her life, and after some time he departed. Then after a couple of weeks, the second one came into her life, too. But the sooner he came, the sooner he left. After it came to pass, she called to ask me who was next in line, but I refused to answer her question; instead, I told her to seek God and to love Him.

Later in 2001, she got saved on her own, two months before I left for the United States. I could not believe it, but God is always wonderful and good all the time, and his promises are truly forever. Today, she is strong in Christ, and God is using her in a mighty way. We communicate very frequently, though we did not get married. We are good friends in Christ and I am proud of her. God wanted to teach me about "love" by making me go through each process of love and rejection. Now I understand what love is and how much I am worth in the eyes of the Lord. It took sacrifice and determination for God to win my heart, glory be to His Holy name.

Today I understand the simple facts and the true meaning of love. Today, I breathe love, I walk in love, I speak love, I think love and I give love. My relationship between God and me is nothing but love. The facts of love that guide me every day are:

- Genuine love does not attach conditions; it is always a free gift to others.

- I believe love sometimes fails for lack of wisdom or from an abundance of weakness, but it forgives, knowing the intentions are good. God never fails, but we fail Him. Love itself does not fail, but we fail love.

- True love, the intimate love, will never reject others. It is the first to encourage and the last to condemn. God is love. He encourages us but does not condemn anyone.

- Love realizes and accepts that there will be times when miles lie between people, but love is a commitment. It believes and ensures all things.

- Love takes time to build. It needs a history of giving and receiving, laughing and crying, sacrificing and suffering.

- True love means believing in someone or in something. It supposes a willingness to struggle, to work, to suffer, to rejoice and to die.

- Love is everything you can do to help others build whatever dreams they have.

- True love involves much careful and active listening. It is doing whatever needs to be done, and saving whatever will promote the others' happiness, security and well-being. But sometimes it hurts, especially when it is rejected.

- Love is a constant journey to what others need. It must be attentive, caring and open, both to what others say and to what others cannot say.

- It is true that unfair treatment may cause survivors to suffer from distress, fear and guilt, and that they need love to heal.

This is my checklist to make sure that I am truly practicing genuine love. The understanding of the above factors helps me to stay in the cause that I was called for. I am not forced to do what is right in the eyes of the Lord nor I do not need to memorize His law. The law has no power over my life because it is a chain of slavery. Knowing and understanding the true meaning of love set me free. The power of love granted me the true liberty in the house of God because I gained favor in the eyes of the Lord. No love, no favor. True love can only be realized through forgiving and appreciation.

> Love helps us to stand in the promises of God no matter what happens to our lives. It is a moving sea between the shores of our souls and God's Spirit.

CHAPTER 10

A VISION OF HEAVEN

In this chapter, I narrate my journey to heaven. I thought since I believed in God and everything is possible in his eyes, that I would like to experience how people feel when they die, and also to visit heaven. I should not fear this, I knew, because God is able to give life and to take it away.

A Journey to Heaven

I humbled myself before God and requested that He allow death to come my way for a couple of hours. One night, I was half-asleep and I saw a vision. I came out of my body and left it behind. What was strange was that the moment I left my body, I found myself in another world, very bright and full of glory. Later I found myself in a beautiful city that was glittering, and the lights were of different colors, like that of a rainbow. The light led me to a special room, where I found the trinity. I was welcomed by one of them, who introduced Himself as God, the creator of the Universe. I was also introduced to Jesus and the Holy Spirit.

We sat down around the table, ready to eat the cake that had been placed upon the table. He explained that the cake was a banquet prepared in heaven for all those who emerge from this world triumphant. Then he took me near the door and showed me another gate on the left before we ate the cake. I was touched, deep in my heart, when I saw thousands of people heading to the left gate. To my astonishment, the multitude was passing God's gate, which was wide open, but none would dare look at it. I was touched when God told me that they were blind (spiritual blindness) and could not see. They had lost their eyes to the things of the world and now they had nothing to talk about except what they used to own in the world.

As I was watched them helplessly, I saw my biological mother with other women, talking and laughing as they passed the gate. I shouted to her, calling her three times, and the third time she turned, looked at me, then continued passing by. I knew where she was heading—the lake of fire was waiting for her. I cried to God to allow her to come in, but He said to me, "Charles, my gate is wide open for anyone who wants to come into my house, but I cannot force anyone to come in. Even after they are dead, I still give them a chance to come back home by leaving my gate wide open. But they are blind and following each other without knowing where they are going." Then He opened a curtain, and I saw a dark, deep hole. The only thing I could hear were the voices of people crying for mercy and help because they could not see anything. I saw my body lying on the bed, but it was rotten. It looked so bad that I did not even want to touch it because I was very clean and dressed in the holy color of white.

Then God the creator said to me, "Charles, we want you to go back to that darkness and bring people to my house. It is empty, and I have prepared a feast for all the people of the world because they are my children." Then I asked him, "What about the cake that is on the table? Why cannot you cut a piece for me?" He said, "No, Charles, first bring my children home from the world of darkness, and then I will allow you to eat as much as you can."

Then I asked him, "How shall I go back in that darkness to bring your children back home, as my body is rotten, too?" He said to me, "Charles, I want you to go back to your body, enter into it, and tell people that the day of the Lord is at hand. The Day of Judgment is coming soon. Tell the people to cleanse themselves by repenting their sins and seeking my kingdom. The time for repenting is now because the night is coming, and they will have no more chances."

I hesitated to leave because I could not imagine that God would refuse to give me a piece of cake to eat, and now He wanted me to go back to the world of darkness and also to go back into my rotten body.

A little while later, I found myself standing next to my body wondering whether it was mine or not, but I fitted myself into it and woke up. What surprised me was that it seemed to me as if I had spent about three days in heaven, but when I woke up it had only been a few hours. I was terrified, and the following weekend I went home to tell my mom to turn back to God by repenting her sins. My mom could not understand what I was telling her because she could not imagine her baby boy as an instrument of God. I went back the following day to Nairobi.

What amazed me about my visit to heaven was that all the people looked alike—they had the same skin color and spoke the same language. Also, when God referred to the world, He did not discriminate against people by color, nation, race, or religion. He simply said to me, "Go to the world and bring my children home." Since then, I have had great respect for all human beings, knowing that we are all children of God and surely our Father is waiting for us all in heaven. I was amazed by God's love for the world. God wants to give us a new name, not to be called the children of the world but the children of God or of the Most High King.

I started praying for my mom and later I was sent two messages. The first one was a prophesy about a stone house that was to be built for her because our house was made of mud, and it was a shame. Neighbors used to laugh at us. This message made my mom laugh, and she thought it was a big joke. The second message was that if she did not repent and turn back to the ways of righteousness, God would allow her to be crushed by the spiritual enemy. Both events came to pass—the house was built, and Mom had a stroke that affected her speech and one side.

Regarding the house, God gave the measurements, the color it was to be painted, and the plan. I was not working, since I was a student, but I was able to organize the family later. They agreed to set up a house so long as it was not a stone one. I stood by God's word, but since I was not contributing anything, I had to agree with them physically. Fortunately, they allowed me to be in charge of the work. My brother gave me the plans, but the mason could not follow it due to unavoidable circumstances. The mason changed the plan, and the changes reflected the house God had given to me in a dream, without approval from the family. They wanted to build a wooden house. When they went home and found that a stone house was being built, and that I was behind the idea, they refused to participate. I prayed to God to bless me with a job in order to accomplish his will. God gave me a job later, and I continued to build the house until it was partially complete.

Regarding the issue of my mom, one night in a vision I saw the Devil coming with his chariots in spirit. I was not at home, but as soon as I saw him surrounding the house, I ran to save our house. When he saw me coming to fight him, fire came from his mouth and nose, pouring upon our house, but I managed to put it off. The fire was spreading faster than I could run. My mom was inside the house and became a victim of spiritual suffocation. I managed to save her, though she was unconscious. A few weeks later, she suffered a minor stroke, but I thank God because now she is okay.

It is true that death does not mark the end of life but the beginning. If we truly believe in Him, then we will live forever with Him in heaven. We are two in one, a soul and a flesh. When the soul leaves the flesh, then the body looks dirty and rotten. No one can agree to come back to life after the soul leaves the body.

CHAPTER 11

ANGEL MESSENGERS

It is true that there are angels all over, but the only reason why we cannot see them with our naked eyes is because of our sins. Angels were created to serve God and man. But due to our ignorance and radical beliefs we tend to ignore their presence. They walk with us, protect us when we are sleeping and bring blessings from God. This chapter illustrates moments with angels.

Angels

I decided that I wanted to see an angel. When I requested that God allow me to see or meet one, He asked me why I was interested, since I had given him a condition not to send me one. One day in the afternoon, I had gone to escort my friend from home in the Nairobi area, and as we were walking, I looked straight up in the sky and I saw an angel floating in the air. He was flying east to west; it was not a dream, but a vision. I was nervous and frightened but courageously I told my friend to look up. She saw something, though he was not as clear to her as he was to me. We departed at a certain point, and I went back home. All along, the angel was still floating up in the sky.

Later, God confirmed to me that He wanted me to have all the time to observe an angel, since I had requested to see one.

This time I was half-asleep and I saw the vision of an angel floating in the air again. He had spread his wings across the sky, covering even the sun. The wings were glittering in different colors. It was very beautiful. In fact, I had never seen such a beautiful creature in my life. I could feel the beauty. He told me that he had come from the Middle East (Greece) to pay a courtesy visit to me, and he was to stay for seven days. Remember, there are four angels at the corners of the world, and this was one of them. I had a wonderful time with him, though He did not inform me when he had to leave.

At another event, my sister sent me to her firm (field) to harvest some potatoes, which she had planted at Nanyuki. In a dream, God told me to make sure the work did not exceed seven days because something was to happen on the seventh day. I went and did according to his instructions, and by the seventh day, everything was in order.

At around 7 p.m., I was still in the field collecting leftover potatoes alone, and it was dark. I looked up, and I saw Jesus with six angels. Two of the angels were on his left side, two were behind him, and two were on the right side, floating in the sky. They did not say a word, but after some few minutes, they disappeared.

During the night, I had a vision whereby the house in which I was sleeping was full of glorious light, and outside there was a huge, long snake that was going around the house looking for a place to get through to come to me. I heard a soft voice that told me not to fear because I was well protected. The Devil (snake) could not touch me because there was no access to the house. I was told to look up, and I saw an arm of a hand over my head; it was producing rays of light, very hot and bright, enough to fill the room, but outside, the house was in total darkness. The voice further told me not to fear because I was under the maximum protection of God, and the snake could do no harm to me.

The snake went around the house three times and then disappeared. What amazed me was that this snake had the name of a person, whom I knew, on its tail. The next day, when I woke up, I was seriously sick. The second day, I had to travel home (Nyeri) to see my parents on my way back to Nairobi. By the time I arrived at home, I could not eat or drink anything. I met our first-born sister Margaret Wangui at home with my parents, and they were shocked to see me in such a state. They asked me to go to the hospital, but I told them not to worry because I had been healed before I fell sick. On the third day, at night, God visited me and healed me completely. The next day we went to cultivate in the field with my sister, and she thought I was a ghost. Then I went back to Nairobi.

This one was during the night: I was on the bed half-asleep. I saw heaven open and a multitude of angels dressed in different colors descended towards me. I saw a king in front of them holding a magic stick, and the angels were singing. Between them and me, there was a very deep, dark valley that had separated us, and in the valley, there was a big river. After reaching the slopes of the valley on the other side, they stopped and kept quiet. I was just standing on the other side, amazed. The king said to me, "Charles, I am Jesus, the son of the living God. We have been sent to you by God to bring to you this magic stick. Since we cannot come over there because the valley is deep and the river is wide, I am going to throw it to you. Do not worry because it will not fall into the valley. It will come dancing. As soon as you hold it, repeat the following words three times: *Ground, open up in the name of Jesus Christ.* The third time, the ground will open, and it will be extremely dark inside. I want you to jump inside, and you will land on the back of a big snake, the Devil. He will be in a deep sleep, so do not fear. Place this magic stick on his back and repeat the following words three times. *Devil, you are defeated in the name of Jesus Christ.* And then come out."

He tossed the magic stick to me. It came on dancing in all directions. I got hold of it and did as I had been instructed to do. I repeated the words three times, and on the third time, the ground opened. There was total darkness inside. I courageously jumped inside without knowing how deep it was but believed and trusted in God. I landed on the back of a very big, sleeping snake. I placed the magic stick on its back and repeated the words three times. After I jumped out. I was very exhausted, and I had to lie down on the surface for a while to recover.

Angels are humble creatures who are always ready to serve and protect us. They are our gardeners. They do not want to see us miserable, sad or doing wrong things. They adore both God and us as long as we live according to God's will.

CHAPTER 12

FAITH

It is a good thing to trust in God because we do not know when our faith is being tested. True trust comes from the heart, not the lips. Faith and trust are built through the long journey of love. Faith must be reflected by actions. The only way to be happy in the Lord is though trusting and obeying His will. In this chapter, I narrate how my faith was tested.

My Faith Tested

God has truly taught me how to trust Him like a small child. One time, when I was attending computer courses, I had to complete three final exam papers. I did the first paper and found it easy. The next day I did the second paper, and it was too hard to understand. I felt so bad because I could not understand why God was with me, yet he could not make it easy for me to understand the paper. Instead of giving thanks and glory to God for at least giving me an opportunity to attend the exams, I became angry and started complaining bitterly all the way home. The whole day I complained because I thought I had already failed the second paper.

That night, I was half-asleep, and I saw myself using a machine to sharpen a knife. As I was sharpening the knife, the knife was moving forward and my right hand was moving, too. I tried to pull my hand away but could not. I heard a voice telling me to save myself since I thought that with my power and strength, I could do so. I ignored the voice because I was very angry, and I said to myself, let me be cut rather than ask for help. My hand was cut into two parts along the center and started bleeding furiously. Then someone approached me, smiling, and said, "I am your God, your Father." He touched my hand, and it was instantly healed. But He said, "Charles, since you have refused to trust in me, I will make you pass the second paper, which you thought you had failed, and fail you in the first paper, which you thought you had passed. I will do this so that you will learn how to trust me. In times of difficulties and in moments of ease, I remain your God and your Father. The circumstances do not change the status of our relationship." He put a big mark on my paper and took my certificate, sprinkling blue ink all over it so that it could not be read. He further said, "Charles, once you get this certificate, you will be required to repeat your exams in order to get a clean certificate that will be legible. This way you will learn how to trust in me."

When I got the results of my test, I found that I had failed paper one and passed all the other exams. I therefore had to repeat the exams in order to get a clean certificate.

Faith Testing

A time came when my faith was to be put to the test. To begin with, I used to teach people about how wonderful it is to have faith and trust in God. God loves and cares for us as individuals. I used to claim that I would do anything that God asked me to do without turning back. One of the most exciting examples I used was this: In the event that God commanded me to go to any overseas country without a penny in my pocket, I would do it. I did not know that I was putting myself to the test.

A time came when I had to go to the United States to further my studies.

In October 1999, my employer decided to lay me off, including a number of other staff members, after closing one of the branches. We were given two months' notice. I continued being faithful and dedicated to my work, though I did not believe in the notice we had been given; I was waiting for further confirmation from God. Late in December, my boss called me and told me to discard the notice because he wanted me back. I told him to give me some time to think about it.

I went home and prayed about it because it was not clear what was going on. To answer my prayers, God showed me a plantation of fruit trees with plenty of fruit that were not ripe. He said to me, "Charles, all these are the blessings waiting for you. I therefore want you to bless your work mate with your job."

The next day, I told my boss that I was not ready to take the offer but instead I wanted to bless my workmate with my position. My boss could not understand what I was talking about. He said, "What?" I repeated the same thing. He said, "Charles, I cannot discuss this with you. I will give you up to the 31st of December to make up your mind."

On the morning of the 31st, I went to my boss's office to give him my final decision. I told him, "Sir, thank you for your kind offer, but I am sorry, I cannot take it; instead, give the offer to my work mate as a New Year blessing." My boss asked me what I was intending to do. I told him I had no plan but was only waiting for what God had in store for me. He could not understand why I had chosen to decline the offer, since getting a job in Kenya at that time was a nightmare. He called the other guy and told him to accept the New Year's gift from me. It was a surprise to him. He came to thank me, but I told him to give thanks to God and to request that God bless me.

I stayed at home in Kenya for a whole year without a job after I obeyed God. I did not bother to ask God why He requested that I give up my job, and yet I was not getting a job. Sometimes I would walk to the city due to the lack of bus fare, but all the time I would glorify His name because I did not want to lose the vision of my blessings.

Seeking University Admission

I had applied to a number of universities in the US, and in April 2000, I received rejections from all the universities. Imagine having no job and no admission to universities, yet still I knew I stood in the promises of God. I trusted in the Lord, and I knew His plans were not our plans. I applied to another university and was admitted in June 2000. I believed God could change a no to a yes. I got my I-20 in June and applied for the Passport, which I received in mid-August. Then I scheduled an American Visa interview, which I was granted on October 5, 2000. I was discouraged because I was supposed to report for school on August 28th, and the I-20 was to expire in September. Therefore, I did not qualify for a Visa that year, and I had to continue staying at home. I requested that the university defer my application, and they agreed.

In December 2000, I happened to pass by my former workplace to say hello to everybody, wishing them a happy and a blessed new year for 2001. I met with everyone, including my boss, who was excited to see me. He told me that he had an opening, and that if I was willing to take it, then he would be happy. I accepted. He offered me a job, which I started in January 2001. At that time, I thought that it would be a good idea to invest the money that I had saved by buying shares in two companies. Within three weeks, before I had gotten the shareholder's certificate, their prices dropped almost by half.

I applied for my Visa and got it in mid-May 2001; therefore, I had enough time to prepare myself. In June, I tried to sell my shares, but there was no one to buy them, and by that time, the price was less than half of what it had been when I'd purchased them. I approached the brokers, but no one was willing to buy, and those who were willing presented bad offers. In July, I agreed with one of my friends that he would give me money, then once the shares were sold, they would be paid into my account and I would transfer the money to his account. He agreed, and I went ahead to do other things, such as buying airline tickets, among other practical things. It was during that time that God instructed me to get a British Visa because he wanted me to visit London.

I woke up very early in the morning to go to the British embassy to apply for a transit Visa. By 10 a.m., I had passed my interview, but I did not have enough money to pay for the Visa since the banks were not open. I requested that the cashier give me about an hour to go to the bank, but instead she told me to come back at 3 p.m. with the payment to get the Visa. At 3 p.m., I had my British Transit Visa.

My departure to the United States was in August 2001, and therefore my flight was on the 17th, with a stopover in London. My friends suggested a get-together or a farewell party before I was to leave. One of my friends, who had promised to bail me out, was in the front line. He went a step further and promised to provide two goats for the occasion.

On the other hand, some family members were not pleased with the idea of me going to the United States.

One day before Saturday, the day of the get-together, we printed invitations and distributed them to our friends. Mysteriously, Mr. B, who was to bail me out, used to be a very close friend to my brother, and nobody knew about it. They had been friends for years, and we were friends, too, but in a different way. In this regard, he was told to leave me alone. He was commanded not to attend the function on Saturday before they met to discuss the issue. They agreed to meet on Saturday afternoon, but in the morning I went with Mr. B to buy goats. He left and promised to be back after meeting with my brother and his friend. During the discussion, Mr. B was warned not to give me any assistance, but no one informed me about it. God revealed this to me before they came. I told Sylvia, a friend of mine who was one of the organizers, what was happening, but she could not believe it. She said I should stop being negative and be positive, but I could not doubt God, no matter what. They came later to the occasion at 8 p.m. when we were dispersing, and I knew things had fallen apart. But my heart was strong because my hope was not built on human strength but on the everlasting rock, The Most High God. Nothing could tremble or shake my faith because I knew my God lives and He is always able to do all things.

The next day, Sunday, I contacted my friend, Mr. B. who had promised to give me money on Monday morning. On Monday, he promised to give me money on Tuesday, and on Tuesday, he promised to give me money on Wednesday morning because the flight was in the afternoon, at 5 p.m.. We agreed to meet at 10 a.m. on Wednesday, but he did not turn up. I waited for two hours at the bank, and then I called Sylvia and Mary at midday, my close friends, and requested that they pray for me. I went to cancel the flight, but the lady said no. "Charles, you have the ticket—go, and you will sort it out yourself later." I went and sat somewhere, ready to see the day passing, taking my dream away. I knew that the moment the day died, it would be the end of my dream as well.

At about 1:30 p.m., God sent Mary with a message to tell me that He was with me, and the flight was waiting for me. She was instructed by God not to leave me and to make sure that I boarded the plane. She called me and requested that I meet her in a certain hotel in Nairobi. I went there, but at that time, I was completely worn out and hopeless. My faith had completely gone, leaving me spiritually blind and empty. Mary gave me the message, but my faith was too low to make me stand or to see clearly since I had become blind; therefore, I could not understand what she was talking about. I told her that she could say what she wanted to say but that I was not leaving Kenya until God proved to me that He would be with me. At about 3 p.m., my heart had softened, and I decided to take a risk because I knew that the worst that could happen to me was death. To me, death is my best friend, and in fact is a solution to all my problems.

We hired a taxi to take us home to pick up my belongings, but unfortunately I had not packed, and the flight was at 5 p.m.. I took what was in the box and left most of my important belongings, including the scripts that I had used to record all the events that God had showed to me and all the teachings that God had taught me. I left home hurriedly, without even taking a shower or changing my clothes. I arrived at the airport at 4:25 p.m. and immediately went to check in since I was the last passenger. I boarded the flight and at 5:30 p.m., it took off.

After flying for more than two hours, I put my earphones on to watch a movie. That is when I heard a soft voice whispering into my ears. I removed my earphones to listen to the voice because I recognized it. The voice said, "Charles, do not worry about where you are going because I am with you. I am your God and my Spirit is everywhere. I have made the way clear for you, and you will never lack anything. Today, you are all alone. No one else can help you, but I am your God, your Father, and I am with you. I created the universe and its inheritance and all belongs to me. America is my place, just as Kenya is my place. I will make it comfortable for you just the way Kenya was. Forget about your country home, Kenya. Now you are heading to America, your new home. Trust me, and I will take good care of you, and you shall glorify me. Do not forget to teach my children in America about my love and the last day that is coming."

He instructed me to call an old friend of mine while at the London airport because He wanted me to encourage her. Then to mark his words, he said, "In August of next year, 2002, you shall be driving your own car." I saw a light blue car, and I was told to receive it, and after that I had an anointing from head to toe that made me feel fresh and encouraged. To me, at the time, I thought I was dreaming, and I thought I was hearing my own voice.

After landing at the Abu Dhabi airport for a stopover, I realized that I had only $200.00 in my pocket, and I had forgotten my purse, which contained my Visa and ATM card, together with all my contacts at home, except for a friend in London whose number I had written in an old diary. At once, despite the sweet encouraging words God had whispered to me a while ago, I had a blackout that shut off my mind. We continued with our flight and arrived at Heathrow airport in the morning. Immediately, I called my friend Joanne, and she responded immediately, though she was surprised because she had not been expecting me. She gave me directions and told me to take a cab. I arrived at her place and found her, though she was not feeling well. She was not working and therefore had no money to buy food. She told me that she had no money to buy food for me, but I told her not to worry since I had $200.00 in my pocket. I knew that God would provide.

We went to the shop in the afternoon to buy food. This reminded me of how I used to tell God that I wanted to be fed like Elijah by wild birds. In the first place, I had a blackout because I thought $200.00 would not be enough, but to God it was more than enough. After two days, I had to proceed with my flight to the United States, but the previous night, I had to shop for her because I did not want to leave her without food. I was left with only £ 50 in my pocket, plus a few coins.

My flight was at 3 p.m. at Gatwick airport, and therefore in the morning I had to board a bus from Heathrow airport to Gatwick. My friend escorted me to Heathrow airport. We stayed at Heathrow airport waiting for a bus. Finally it came, but by the time I arrived at Gatwick, it was about 3 p.m. and it was too late to board my flight. I was given a waiver for that day. I left my luggage and went back to Heathrow to spend the night at Joanne's place once more.

The next day, we woke up very early in the morning, and I managed to get a bus around 11 a.m. There was a heavy traffic jam because it was a banker's holiday, and at the same time there was an accident. I arrived a few minutes past 3 p.m.. The supervisor looked at me, shook his head, and gave me another waiver. He asked me whether I could spend the night at the airport, but I said no. I went back to Joanne's house and by then I had only a few coins left since each return ticket was £ 25.

I went back to Joanne's with no money to take me back to the airport the next day. I told Joanne that I did not have bus fare for the next day. I'd spent all the money that I had, and I did not have money to take me to the airport the third day.

Joanne's aunt had invited her for dinner that day, but Joanne called her and told that I was back. The aunt told her to go with me. We met her aunt with another lady by the name Wairimu. Joanne's aunt gave me BP 20 and Wairimu gave me £ 20 too. Wairimu told me that while she was praying, God instructed her to carry £ 20 because He wanted to bless someone. Then later after dinner we went back home. I gave my friend Joanne BP 10 to buy food, and I was left with £ 30.

The next day, I woke up, took a bus to Gatwick airport, and arrived at 1 p.m.. I was the first one to check in, and I waited until 2:30 p.m. when we were told to board the plane. I was scared due to the repeated dreams that I had had, but I had to go anyway.

Every night I asked God what the reason was that I could not seem to make the flights on time. But every night, I could see planes crashing into buildings, shattering into pieces, and bursting into flames in the sky, killing all on board, including myself and those in the building. Most of the people in the plane died due to suffocation and a lot of heat, not the crash. The heat that I could feel in the plane and the screaming of the people dying remains a fresh nightmare to this day. I was a bit concerned because I thought I would be a victim, and not make it to the United States; therefore, I had told Joanne about what I saw. She told me not to worry because it was just a dream, but I could not be convinced, since the dream was repeated twice. Then the events of 9/11 took place.

I finally boarded the flight, took off, and I was on my way to the United States with only $30 in my pocket, after converting it from pounds. After arriving in Boston, I called Mr. Kamau, whose information I had been given in the UK in case I needed help, and he responded immediately. He said he would send a friend of his to pick me up from Logan airport, who would take me to Kamau's home. He asked me what I looked like, and within twenty minutes, his friend Kibathi was there with me. He drove me to Kamau's home, where I waited for him to come home from work. I spent the night at his place, and the following morning he took me to Brandeis University. I reported at school, and I was given the key to my room because the university had residences. Mr. Kamau gave me twenty dollars, and now I felt very rich because I had a total of fifty dollars.

I shopped the next day with my roommate, who was very kind and understanding. I was left with no money. I told my roommate that I did not want to overspend because I did not have enough money but would be getting some very soon from home. To him, he thought I was referring to Kenya, but I meant from heaven.

One Saturday morning, we went to the shopping center with a group of students. I was very hungry but did not have any money to buy food, and my heart was crying for the Lord all the way through. I was praying throughout asking for God's mercy and favor at least to feed me. My friends bought food, but I told them that I did not feel like eating anything because I did not have money. When I went back to the university dorm, I opened the door and found a folded piece of paper with my name on it. I unfolded it and found 20 dollars from my friend Kamau. He had come to see me but could not find me. I was so happy and grateful to my Lord. In fact, to me it was like thousands of dollars because I was frustrated and desperate, but I knew my life was in the hands of God. My eyes were looking unto heaven upon God for mercy. I knew my help could only come from God, no one else.

I had tried to call my friend Kamau earlier, but the phone kept going to voice mail. I was very happy, and filled with joy and praises. I went to buy bread to eat, and my soul was strong.

Now it was the end of August, and classes had started. I decided to wait upon the Lord because I knew God was always in His business of performing miracles, but He never hurries or comes late. He has taught me about punctuality, and patience pays. It was during that time that I met James, a Kenyan who was working at the Brandeis bookstore. I asked the manager whether she could give me a job, but she showed me a stack of applications. Then, after a moment, she came back to me and told me to report the next day at 9 a.m. The next day I reported to the bookstore at 9 a.m., completed the paper work, and started working the same day.

Now I was very rich because I was expecting to receive a check after two weeks. I was able to buy food and other items. That was the way God fed me, like Elijah in the wilderness.

God is always in His business of performing miracles for us, if only we trust and obey His word. He is faithful and never fails. He creates ways where there is no way. He provides water in the desert and makes plants grow there. There is no burden that He cannot help us to lift up, no valley that He cannot reach, no mountain that He cannot climb, no river that He cannot cross, because He is God and everything is possible. In God we trust and everything is possible to us.

CHAPTER 13

DEALING WITH THE DARKNESS

We cannot ignore that the Devil also lives. We have to acknowledge that he exists and is our spiritual enemy. We cannot assume that he does not exist, but how we fight against the Devil and his followers in the power of the darkness depends on us. God taught me how to fight the Devil and also to realize and appreciate the maximum protection God has granted to us.

Confrontation with Satan (the Devil)

Truly speaking, as the Lord God almighty lives, the Devil also lives. In fact, one of the factors that made me believe in the existence of God was the fact that the Devil is alive. I used to read many books written by the agents of the Devil and about devil-worshipping practices. In Kenya, devil worship was very common by then, and many people were believed to have acquired their wealth through devil worship in return for the sacrifice of their own loved ones, such as a wife, a child, a relative, or a friend. In fact, there were several cases (rumors) of events that took place in Kenya, especially involving accidents in various parts of the country, but it was worse in Nairobi and Mombasa.

In 1990, I happened to go to Mombasa, the second largest city in Kenya, for a four-day visit. I had an opportunity to intermingle with people from the coast, or Pwani. A person from the highlands believes that in Mombasa, "gins" behave like human beings, but they are satanic. I asked one of my friends to explain to me about the issue of gins. He said to me, "Charles, gins are real. If anyone tells you there are no gins, they are lying to you. We treat them like pets, but they feed on human blood. They are kept in one of the rooms in a house. The room must be very clean and perfumed. They are inherited from one generation to another by the first-borns, and they have power to change to any form. The purpose of keeping them is because they give us wealth and protection. They can be sent to kill someone, and do so. If not taken care off, they might kill the owner." I asked him whether it was possible to see them, and he told me that it was very possible. One of the guys said, "Charles, if you are interested, I can take you to my house on the outskirts to see them. My father used to keep them, and I was supposed to inherit them since I am the oldest son in the family, but I declined to take the offer; instead, they were inherited by my uncle."

This testimony strengthened my faith and answered many of my questions. Surely I was convinced that if the Devil does indeed exist, God does, too. When I went back to Nairobi, I had more faith, strength, and a new vision of my destiny. I made a commitment to myself that I must beseech God, the creator of the universe. I was determined that no matter what was ahead of me, all that I desired was to know God and to establish a good relationship with Him. I wanted to walk with Him day-by-day. I tried to imagine how bored and lonely God might be, since we do not keep him company. I wanted to be his best friend, to walk with him and kill his boredom. On the other hand, the Devil was not impressed with my determination. As I was thinking about God, the Devil was thinking about me. As I was thinking about how to build a relationship with God, the Devil was thinking about how to destroy my relationship with God.

After I met God, the Devil was not left behind. One time God warned me in a dream to be careful and not to believe every vision or dream or voice, because not all of them came from Him. The Devil is in spirit, and he can mimic an angel of God. He is a spiritual being and therefore has the ability to change form. He can appear in the form of lights or even as an angel; furthermore, he is a rebellious angel, but God instructed me on how to identify those belonging to Him.

One night, I was lying in bed half-asleep, and a bright light filled my room. Two gentlemen appeared to me in white robes, and one said to me, "Charles, we have been sent by God almighty, your Father, to come for you. He wants you to be with him, and we are His servants. Will you come with us please?" Being excited I said, "Sure, why not. I am so delighted and thankful." I immediately left my body. They put me in the middle, and then we started walking in spirit away from my body down the hill. As soon as we had walked for a distance, I heard a voice calling me from behind. I turned my head to see who was calling me back, and I saw God with a very bright light calling me up the hill. He said, "Charles, come back. Do not go with them because I did not send them. They are not my angels." By the time I turned my head to look at them, they had run away in a different direction. To my surprise, they were no longer wearing white robes; they were changing into different, ugly creatures, such as pigs, skeletons, and warthogs. I went back and fitted myself into my dirty, rotten body again.

In 1993, I intended to travel upcountry for a couple of days. Three days before the day of departure came, I saw the vision of a very big snake lying under my bed. In the evening, I had to pray before going to bed. I declared to the Devil that, whether he liked it or not, I had to go home because he had no power or authority to touch me. I further told him that if I died, it would be because of God's will. I further said, "Devil, you'd better be a bit reasonable because my death would not benefit you at all. My soul belongs to God, and my death will not mark the end of the fight between you and me. In fact, it will mark the beginning of a new fight because I will be in spirit, like you. I will fear you no more. I will be able to chase you anywhere in the land, sea, under the world, above the sky. In other words, anywhere you go, I will chase you there because you and I will be in the same form. Going to the grave is not the end but the beginning of a new and a better life. Death will open a door for me to enter into the kingdom of my Father. Shame on you, Devil."

The next day, I woke up very sick, with my chest aching. I visited three different health clinics. Within forty-eight hours, I had taken 107 tablets (pills) and nothing had changed. Instead, I was becoming worse. I took the remaining pills to the toilet, flushed them away, and waited for death to come. I then believed that if it was the will of God, then I would live, but if not, I should not fight death. Since then I have never visited a hospital for treatment or taken any pills, except for dental work. This is not because I do not fall sick; in fact, I fall sick more frequently, but I believe I am the caretaker of the true church of God, my body. My responsibility is to inform the owner of the church (my body) that things are not in order, and I do not have to worry about my body. It is no longer my body but a house of God. I believe God knows the cause(s) of my sickness, and I should let Him take control.

The night of the day I was to travel home, I had a vision, and I heard a voice telling me that I would die in an accident. I even saw my body lying somewhere along the road after the accident. When I woke up, I recognized that the message was not from God but from the Devil, who was planning to kill me. The snake was still under the bed, and I could see it with my naked eyes, though it was in spiritual form.

The day I had planned to go home was on Thursday. I woke up very early in the morning. I said goodbye to everyone in the house, as I thought it might be my last moment with them. I boarded the passengers' vehicle (a Nissan Matatu) at 8:30 a.m., and I sat in the front seat with the driver. The Matatu left Nairobi at 9 a.m. to upcountry Mukurwe-ini, Nyeri. As soon as we left the city center, on the Muranga-Thika road highway, I saw an angel ahead of us high in the sky. I knew God was with me and that nothing bad could happen to me. The journey was safe.

There were two stages that I could take, but either one would require that I take another vehicle home. I decided to take the longer route to give the Devil a greater chance to prove his words. I arrived in my hometown at around 12 noon and found Mom at the shopping center. When she saw me, she became worried because I looked tired and weak, and my face had become pale. She gave me money to go to a restaurant, but I did not take it because I could not eat anything. I asked her for the house key because all that I wanted was to go home to sleep, since I was seriously ill and weak, with a persistent headache.

As I was approaching home, my eyes opened, and I saw someone standing, leaning on a tree near the house, facing the house. I knew it was a ghost or gin; the same snake that had been under my bed was now ahead of me. I arrived at home, passed it, opened the door, and then locked the room from the inside. Though it was a wooden house, I could see clearly outside through the wooden gaps. I did not fear because I knew I had the maximum protection of God, since I belonged to the most and mighty king, the creator of the universe.

As soon as I went to bed I fell asleep because I was weak and tired. It did not take long before the same ghost appeared in my dreams with a message that I was going to die. I did not say a word, but deep in my heart, I had made up my mind not to deny God, whether I died or not. I believe that to live is a privilege, and death is a promotion from one glory to another because it can open the doors of heaven and let me into my Father's home. It would fulfill my heart's desire because it had been my desire to go and live with my savior, my Lord Jesus Christ.

The evening came, and my mom came back and prepared dinner, but I could not eat. My face had turned dark, and I was shivering. She asked me why I had come all the way from Nairobi if I was sick, instead of going to the hospital. She also suggested that she could call neighbors to take me to the hospital. I told her not to worry because even if I went to the hospital, a doctor or a nurse could do nothing for my case. She started crying because she knew I might not make it the next day, though she could not argue with me. At that time, she knew God was with me, and my case was beyond human comprehension.

I went back to my room to sleep without telling her about the ghost outside because I did not want to scare her, and anyway, she could not see it. I slept the whole night, and my mom called me early in the morning at 6 a.m. to find out whether I was still alive. I woke up and took tea without milk or sugar, because all that I wanted was something bitter. Later, my mom left to go to the shopping center where she was operating a grocery store. I stayed at home alone, with the ghost still in the same position, still unmoving, just gazing at me. In the evening, my mom came back early because she was worried, but it was just a matter of time, because I had grown weak and ill since I was not eating, and the ghost was still sucking my blood. I just took tea without milk, then went to bed. I left my mom crying for her son because I did not want to see her shedding tears for me while my heart was overflowing with joy and peace because I knew God was on my side.

That night, at midnight, I was half-asleep, shivering, and I thought it was my last moment on earth. I wanted to wake up and call my mom to say goodbye, but I could not move my body—I was paralyzed. Then, after a while, the room was filled with bright light, and it became very hot; I knew my God, my Father, had come to rescue His child. I heard a soft voice talking to me. "Charles, do not worry because the Devil and his agents of darkness have no power over your life. He can try to harm your body from a distance, but he cannot touch you. Charles, I want you to turn and face the ghost or gin, stretch your hands directly to it, and rebuke it in the name of Jesus Christ."

I did that, and immediately the beams of light radiated from my hands, consuming the ghost completely, and I was healed instantly. After that, I felt fresh, warm, hungry, and thirsty.

The next morning, I woke up early, at around 6 a.m. I went to the field (Shamba) to plant maize because it was planting season in the month of March. When my mom woke up, she went to my room but found that the door was locked from the outside. She panicked because she thought that my dad had discovered I was dead and locked the door from the outside before she found me. She shouted my name, and I heard her from the field. I answered her while in the field, busy digging traces (lines) and planting maize. She came closer until she could see who was answering. When she saw me, she could not believe her eyes; she almost collapsed. She thought that I was another ghost. I was strong, and my face was shiny, covered with the glory of God. She prepared breakfast, and then called me to take my breakfast. She made eggs, slices of bread, and tea with milk, and I ate it all.

My mom was scared and did not want to touch or come close to me. She asked me what had happened that I had been instantly healed. I replied to her, "My God healed me last night," without explaining in detail. She also asked me why I was planting when the rain had not yet started. I said to her, "Mom, do not worry, my God has the key to the source of rain. My work is to plant, and His work is to send the rain and make the seed grow." Actually, people were waiting for the long rain to start in order to start planting. I continued planting maize, and my mom did not go to open the grocery store that day. She decided to stay at home with me because she thought she was dreaming and maybe I could disappear any time.

It took me about two days to plant, and the third day I went back to Nairobi. Before I left, I narrated the whole story to her regarding the cause of my illness, and she was scared to death. I told her about the ghost and how God had healed me. What I learned from this story is that God does not fight for us, but He gives us the power and authority needed to fight and defeat the Devil. Trusting in Him is an assurance that the miracles of victory will always be on our side.

The House of the Devil

Another time, I requested God to take me to Satan's place where he lives and to show me his home. One night, as I was sleeping, the spirit of God took control of me, and I left my body. I found myself in another world, under the world, where the Devil lives. I saw a very big mansion that was very beautiful, but not complete. In the compound, the workers were very busy planting trees and flowers of all different kinds. Inside the house, there were live flowers planted, and fishponds. There was a stream of water that was flowing around the house to water the flowers. It was a very beautiful house outside.

The house was well guarded, right from the gate. The gatekeeper opened the gate for me, because I was dressed like them, and allowed me in. I went and joined other workers who were very busy. I visited the house both inside and outside. As I was very busy visiting the rooms, the Devil called for an urgent meeting in the conference room. Among the workers, two of them were there by mistake, because I could see their hearts were not dedicated to serving the Devil, and they were looking for an opportunity to escape.

We all gathered in the conference room, and soon the king of darkness, Satan, or the Devil started addressing us with a lot of anger. He started by saying that there was an intruder or a stranger among us. At once, I looked at myself and found that I was the only one dressed in white, while the rest were in black. I knew I was not safe at all, and the only option I had was to use force. I jumped and got hold of the two individuals I had identified earlier; I held their hands side by side, and then we ran away towards the gate.

The agents and the demons at first were confused because they did not know what was happening. After we ran away, they were instructed to follow us. The gatekeeper closed the gate. We went with full force, kicked the gate and we passed through. They were very cooperative. Behind us, we were followed by the workers who left all that they were doing to run after us. No conference took place. Now, some of those workers were changing to monsters, pigs, and dogs in order to scare us. We reached a certain point, and then we could go no further, since we were exhausted. I turned back and started rebuking the agents of the Devil in the name of Jesus Christ. Beams of light started glowing from my hands, which destroyed most of them. The rest stopped coming towards us and later turned back. The two guys were agents of the Devil, but I thanked God because He saved them even when they were serving the Devil in his own house. My mission had been to go and rescue them.

Fighting with the Devil

One day I felt sick and became angry at the Devil. By the way, whenever I fall sick, I do not disturb God, praying for healing, but rather I request permission and power to fight with the Devil. Falling sick is my spiritual strength. I specifically went to the Ngong hill to give a sermon to the Devil, but not to pray. I went there for overnight prayers and to declare a war against the Devil. I asked permission from God to allow me to challenge the Devil or Lucifer in the field, spiritually, at midnight the following day. Then the next morning, I went home and went about my normal activities. During the night, I was half-asleep, and I saw the light in my room; then I heard a voice telling me to wake up. I saw the Devil pleading with God not to grant me permission. I became angry, and I challenged him in front of God. I asked God to give me permission to fight with the Devil by betting my own life. I promised God that if I defeated the Devil, then he should move to the sea to live there. Likewise, in case the Devil defeated me, then I should die and no longer live in this world (on the mainland). In either case, one had to leave the mainland. God granted me permission, and then I woke up.

I went back to sleep, and the spirit of God took control of me. I found myself in another world. There was nothing except beautiful green grass, and dark clouds covered the sky and natural, beautiful lights, though there was no sun, moon or stars. I knelt down to pray, and before I said a word, I was knocked down by the Devil. He had the power to appear and disappear into thin air. I was watching him from the east, and he could appear from the west; I could watch him from the north, but he could appear from any direction. At the same time, there was an irritating noise from the dark clouds that disturbed me, and I could not stand it. When I was almost ready to give it up, I called out the name of God to give me power and the ability to fly and disappear like the Devil. It was given, and I was able to fly and disappear into the clouds. I woke up very exhausted, and I refused to accept defeat. I asked God to give me another chance, which he did. After a few minutes, I fell asleep again, and the Spirit of God took control of me and led me to the same battlefield. We continued fighting, though now we were fighting in the sky. After chasing each other, I remembered that I was being defeated because I had forgotten to use the most powerful weapon, to rebuke the Devil in the name of Jesus Christ. The Devil does not want to hear this name being mentioned because he automatically becomes powerless. I therefore began to rebuke him in the name of Jesus Christ, and at once I saw him falling down from the sky. I ran after him. I knocked him down; he hit the ground and broke his two legs.

When I woke up, I gave thanks and glory to the living God for the victory because it was not my victory but his victory. Within three days, I saw fire burning on the surface of the ocean, without consuming the water. Accidents in the ocean began taking place one after the other, starting with that of the Mutongwe ferry at Mombasa. I prayed to God to cover the ocean with the precious blood of Jesus. The Devil chooses to go to the ocean because there are no people praying in the ocean or praying for the ocean. Therefore, it was naked, and that is why he went there.

Queen of the Sea

One day the spirit of God took me into the world under the sea where the Queen of the sea lives. I arrived there at the time the mass service was about to start, and the Queen of the sea was the one who was conducting the mass service. There were many people in the front, and therefore I stood behind them. Most of them were wearing green robes, but all were dressed in the way that bishops dress.

There were many people attending the mass service, and no one could recognize me since the rest of us were dressed casually. They were burning frankincense and myrrh, and everywhere smelled good. There was a very beautiful, natural light, but it was not from the sun or moon. The mass service was to be conducted in the field, and the ground was covered with a beautiful, green grass. As soon as the Queen of the sea approached the altar, which was built outside, she turned, faced the crowd, and then noted my presence. She became angry and shouted, "There is an intruder, and he must be brought to me before we conduct the mass service." At once I saw myself different from the others because a ring of light surrounded me. I knew my life was in danger, and therefore I took off, running away for my safety. The guards were told to run after me. When I saw them coming, I stopped, turned to them, and I told them not to touch me. They stopped. I started rebuking them in the name of Jesus Christ, and they all stopped and then turned back. I walked back home through a tunnel, leaving them stranded, though they were changing into different, ugly creatures to scare me. The Queen of the sea was disgusted because she could not understand how I had come in without being noticed by anyone. Where did I get all that power, she wondered. She was amazed.

This vision reminded me about the scripture noting that when God called a meeting in heaven, the Devil was together with the sons of God. No one else noted his presence except God Himself. This scripture is in the book of Job in the Bible. That is how I attended her service, but no one recognized me except her.

Wedding with the Queen of the Sea

On another occasion, I was asleep and a man appeared to me in my dream. He told me to go with him because there was something he wanted to show me. He pressed a button, and a door opened, similar to that of a lift (elevator). Within a second, we were walking in the streets of a certain city. To my surprise, we stopped at a cemetery. Then at once we found ourselves before a house that looked like a palace. There were many people in this palace who were dressed in the same way; I was the only one who was dressed differently.

The pavement was decorated with flowers, and seated at the high table was a beautiful woman, the Queen of the sea. She was seated there wearing a wedding gown. On her right hand, there was an unoccupied chair. When she saw me, she stood up, called me by my name, and invited me to go and sit in the reserved seat next to hers.

As soon as I sat down, she introduced me to the council as her husband-to-be, and an old man within the council was told to conduct the wedding ceremony, despite the fact that I was not in wedding attire. As he started conducting the ceremony, he told me to swear and make vows to the bride, but I refused. I told them that I had no commitment to make, that it was the bride who should make the commitment to love me. When I became stubborn, she became angry and ordered me to be taken into custody. At that time, a ring of light came and surrounded me, and I walked away without being touched by anyone. They all kept silent and created a way for me to pass. The Holy Spirit of God took me back to my rotten and dirty body.

The World under the World

One day I wanted to discover the world under the world. I was half-asleep when the spirit of God took control of me. I found myself walking in the streets of a town that did not have a sun or a moon. There were roads, electricity, and everything else similar to what we have here. In that world, the people were extremely busy. I toured various factories that made things such as fragrance and clothing. I asked the gentleman who was taking me for a tour what they were for. He said to me, "They were made to confuse people in the real world so that they can easily respond to the power of the Devil or darkness. If people were not confused, they would not listen to us. They would follow God and do what pleases God, and therefore we would have no followers."

At that time, we arrived at another factory, and nearby there was a big dam full of sewage water. The water was stagnant and producing a bad odor. It was greenish in color. I asked what it was for, and I was told, "It is used to create diseases and sickness to infect the humans. If people did not have problems, we could not trap them. Sickness and disease deprive people of peace and love. This is a good weapon or trap because through it we trap millions of people. The majority of people die without repenting their sins. We know that God hates anyone who dies without repenting because he or she does not qualify to go to heaven to live with God."

I asked him why they did that to human beings. He said, "God loves mankind very much, and he made man like him. He has given man unlimited power and authority over the whole world to control, but the angels were given none, though they have been here before man. Our work is to separate man from the love of God because man is ignorant of God's existence. Man cannot stand on his own, though he does not know that. We know that man is weak because of his flesh, and we are strong because we are in spirit. We take advantage because we know more about God and man. We know man's destiny and ours, too. We do not force man to follow us, but man is greedy and selfish. He is like God and has the ability to do many things that we cannot do. But man does not understand himself, nor does he understand God, and therefore he does not understand where he came from or where he is heading. He does not make use of his ability. He has the power and authority over everything God created in this world, including us, but due to his foolishness, he walks blindly with no hope. We made him a slave, though he is a king. We are supposed to be under his feet, but he is under our feet.

"God has blessed man with unlimited power and authority, yet he is crippled. God Himself is generous with His power. No one knows where God gets His power because if we need power and go to Him, He always provides us with it. We do respect God because He is our source of power, but we do not acknowledge Jesus as the king chosen by God to rule in His kingdom. Our work is to make sure man will not inherit the kingdom of God because we want to perish with him. If man could only understand himself, he would need less from God because God has given him power and authority to be independent, and all that he needs to do is to open up to release those powers and we are done."

Then he took me into a building where the drugs and diseases were being processed inside a room that was very hot. He locked the door and disappeared, leaving me there to die. After reviewing their secrets, I was not supposed to come back to the real world. I was to die and be changed so that I was like them, but God was great because he saved me. An angel from God appeared from nowhere, held my hand, and led me out by creating a way where there was no way, and finally I came back to the real world.

Our power or strength cannot save us or give us victory over the power of the darkness. We need to put on our armor for protection. The name of Jesus Christ, our Lord and savior is the spiritual supernatural weapon; and the blood that he shed on Calvary is our armor.

CHAPTER 14

ON PREPARING FOR DEATH

This is a vision I had about my last day on earth. In this vision, my last day came to pass. The angels came for me, but I was not prepared. When this happened, I could understand what I was thinking about after leaving this world. The news spread about my death and the funeral preparations began.

My Last Day

One time in 1994, I started praying for my last day. One night I had a vision of my last day on earth. These first two paragraphs are my thoughts after the vision was over. If I had known that tomorrow would not be mine, I would have beseeched God with all my heart. I did not know that a day would come when I would see neither the sunrise nor the sunset. There would be nothing around me except dust. All my friends and relatives would be no more. I would look around, but the only thing I would see would be dust. The sun would rise as usual to open the day, but I would not be aware that it would be my last day in this bitter, ungraceful world. I did not know that life was meant to be so short, that it was meant for cleansing or preparing myself for a Holy land, but not to eat or to drink or to enjoy life.

I thought and convinced myself that the world was my destination. I forgot the purpose that God had for me in this world, and instead I did all that was pleasing to my heart and flesh. I could not understand that beyond this life I was living, there was another, better life to come. To the best of my knowledge, I thought that the life of a human being started from the womb and ended in a tomb. I did not want to know or believe that God existed and lived forever. I did not know that there is a beautiful and glorious dwelling place, heaven, and that it is the dwelling place of God. The angels and the holy ones worship and praise God in that beautiful place. In that Holy place of God, there will be no more tears, sickness, sadness, death, anger, jealousy, or adultery. Only goodness will be found in that land, and the glory of God is enough to be the light and healing of nations. The presence of God in that city will comfort, give hope, and heal all those with wounded hearts. God will wipe their tears of grief and instead give them the tears of joy. He will serve them the cake that was prepared for them before the creation of the world. God will give them a warm welcome hug as a sign of love between the son and daughter and the Father. He will not only be their God, but He will also be their loving and caring Father. The first love that was there in the Garden of Eden shall be restored, and the gap that was created as a result of sin will be no more. God will review the many things to them that He has kept in secret, since the creation of the world.

It was during the night, when I was half-asleep, that finally, my big moment came. I did not prepare for it in advance because I was already lost in the confusion of the world, wondering and doubting whether there was a God. At that time in my life, to the best of my knowledge, I would define God as a monster that exists somewhere without any form, but I could care less because I never knew that God knew me by my name. It never occurred to me that He cares and loves me.

When the hour to graduate from the human level to the spiritual level comes, it means to die. I saw a spaceship, painted green, coming towards me. It came to where I was lying on the bed. There were two gentlemen inside wearing white robes. They told me to board, but I started looking around to see who could talk to them to allow me at least another day. I asked them where they were taking me, and when I would be able to come back. I was shocked when they said, "Charles, your life in this world is over, and now you must come with us. You have no more life to live in this world. You are going forever and are never coming back again." This meant that I had no credit left on my time card.

I asked them to grant me permission to bid a word of goodbye to all those I loved, including my parents, sisters, brother, nieces, nephews, relatives, and friends—the list was too long. One of the gentlemen said to me, "Charles, you had all the time to say anything to all those you loved since the day you were born. What have you been waiting for? Were you not prepared for this big day?"

I replied, "No, sir." I asked him how I was supposed to prepare for this day. He smiled at me, and said, "Charles, this world is a continuous journey (transition) to another beautiful city where we (angels) live. Each and every day of your life is a day for preparation for this big day. Do not wait for tomorrow; do it today because today is yours but tomorrow belongs to God. As you were praying every day, you were supposed to pray for this big day so that God would prepare it for you. God prepared your day to be born, but it is up to you to prepare for your last day in this world. God could have shown you that we were coming for you today, but you never wanted to accept that you would leave this world. That is why you have been caught unawares. By the way, when you came into this world, you did not inform anyone that you were arriving, and likewise, you do not have to inform anyone that you are about to leave. The journey was meant for you alone and your God."

At that time, both of them alighted from the vehicle. One took hold of my left hand and the other one took hold of my right hand. They helped me to stand up (my soul left the body), and I walked with them to the spaceship. We boarded and took off. Even after taking off, I was still connected with my dirty and rotten body, but at this time I was in another world. Then the spaceship stopped, and one of the gentlemen told me to watch what was going to happen to my body.

The shocking news began to spread across the country like a burning bush that "Oh, Charles is no longer with us." All those who highly regarded my name began to grieve. They were sobbing, trying to imagine where I could be and how I might be feeling. I could understand their thoughts, hear their conversations, but they could not see me. My rotten body was taken and preserved in a funeral home, well taken care of, washed twice a day, dressed properly, and sprayed with the most expensive perfume. I felt so bad and pitied them because I could not understand why they were bothering with my rotten body.

The day for the funeral came, and many mourners came to see me for the last time, carrying bouquets of flowers. I was dressed in very expensive clothes, put in an expensive coffin, and driven in an expensive van. What surprised me was that among the mourners, there were some who had nothing to eat, no proper dress, and nowhere to sleep. I was not happy about it because the total expense for my funeral could have catered to their needs. I felt ashamed because I could see myself as a selfish person. The poor people who happened to be my friends were treating my body like a king, contributing all that they had. The two gentlemen looked at me as I was struggling to answer many questions within myself. I thought, *why could not they treat me like a poor person since I am no longer with them, and instead treat themselves like kings?* At that time, I could not hold it any longer. I asked the gentlemen to explain to me why my relatives and friends were doing this for me.

One of the gentleman said to me, "Charles, no one among them believes that today is your day and tomorrow is their day, in order to prepare themselves. They believe that once you die it is the end of you. If they could understand that there is life after death, they could be worshipping and praising the Lord because you have gone. Your departure could be a sign to all that their last days are drawing near, too, and therefore they need to be ready. Now they are all confused and blind, just doing the work of sending you to the grave forever. To them, they do not think that tomorrow they will be in the same position you are in today. To the best of their knowledge, death is nothing but an accident. That is why they are spending a lot of money to console themselves—not because they loved you. If you should return to life, they would run away and tell you to go back to the dead. Why, do they really love you?"

I thought about it, and it was true that they were not doing these things out of love but simply to follow customs.

After that, I saw the procession from the funeral home heading to where I had been born. As they were about to arrive, I saw a very beautiful building surrounded with flowers and natural light, but not of the sun. It had a flag with Jesus at its top and the angels were going in and out of the building. Inside, the building was painted white and the carpet was white, too. I could not believe it when I saw the procession heading to that building. The people alighted from their cars, and the coffin that had my remains was pulled out of the van. People who wanted at least to touch me for the last time, because they did not want to believe I was heading to the grave, offered to carry my coffin. They proceeded into the main door of the building. The angels, who were very busy going in and out, took to their heels when they saw my coffin. The glory that was covering the building also left the building. At once the building was left naked, and now I could see the benches and the dirty floor. The priest in charge conducted the funeral services and later the coffin was taken out of the church to the graveside.

At the graveside, the coffin was lowered into the grave and thereafter covered with the soil. In fact, the guys who were doing the job did not care that I might be feeling pain or coming back to life. After everything was done, my relatives and friends laid flowers on the grave and left for their homes. After about one hour, there was no one near the grave, and I found my remains all alone. I did not see anyone volunteering to be with me or to be left in the graveyard. The night came when everyone went to sleep, and I was forgotten outside. That was the time when I realized that it is true that I came to this world alone and I will leave alone. In this world, the best you can get from your relatives and friends is a good and honored burial ceremony that is later forgotten, but God will never leave you. Whether at the time of death or in the grave, He will always be there for you. He will welcome you to His kingdom.

What I learned was that God does not like us to spend a lot to pay last tributes to our relatives and friends while those around us are starving. It would have been better if the donations collected were used to feed the needy ones who had attended my funeral. Also, God is not happy to see the remains of humans taken to the church because it defiles the Holy Place of God. It is like emptying a carton of milk but then continuing to keep the empty carton in the refrigerator.

Each of us needs God, no matter what or who we are. God remains supreme, and our creator. The life in this world is too short. Imagine that few people live to see the beauty of the sunrise or sunset more than 36,500 times (the equivalent to 100 years) from the time of birth to death. God is calling you to protect you and to give you eternal life.

We can run short of God's glory and grace, but we cannot run short of God's love. His love is unconditional in spite of our iniquities at the time we are alive. But when death comes, it is over.

The vision teaches me that we need to be prepared for our heavenly departure. It is true that when we die, it is not the end of our lives but beginning of a new live. Death is inevitable but we need to be aware of it. But we tend to ignore it and when it comes it always find us unaware and unprepared. God is waiting to cleanse us and prepare the day of departure if only we request Him to do so through prayer.

Last Prayer

Thank you God for the time you have given me to live in this merciless and bitterness world. Lord I cannot complaint for anything because you have blessed me from the time I came to this world until this day when I am leaving it. It was through your grace and favor that I am the way I am. Many were born with various disabilities, including mental and physical health. Many went without food, drinks or clothing, but for me you had provided well. Millions have died through various causes but you have kept me alive until this day. I have seen the glory of sunrises and sunsets for all those days.

Lord, I glorify your name because you have been my refuge. When strong winds and floods came I leaned on you. Lord, you have never forsaken or rejected me. Though sometimes, Lord, it was not easy for me, sometimes I was crying, sometimes I was sad, sometimes depressed or in dithery moods, but God, you would send a sign of love, a heart or green apple to remind me that you are still with me. Your encouragement lifted me up; sometimes it could make me pass through fire without burning. You have never left me around my enemies as they celebrate their victory or laugh at me. But you prepared a table for me in the presence of my enemies to eat and drink and watch you fighting for me. The fight has never been mine, but ours. When I was sick you could give me medicines or touch my chest and get healed. You made me see light in the midst of darkness.

Lord, you have made my dreams come true. You have made me keep my promise with you. Lord, as I come to my last sunset, let me go in peace. Let that day be the most beautiful day in my life. Let the sky be clear and may the world receive your peace and glory in that week you will come for me. Let me know in advance three days before that you are coming for me; be specific with day, hour and minute. Lord, when I take my last breath I would like to commit my soul unto your holy hands. Lord, open my eyes seven days before so that I will enjoy seeing your glory, the new heaven and heavenly bodies. Lord, I want to see bright light when my eyes close to death.

Lord, prepare this glorious day for me. Let it be the day you will have less to do. I want you to come for me, but please do not send angels. I am your child, a friend and a servant. I want you to introduce me to heavenly bodies but not to have angels introduce me to you. I am leaving this earth to go home, to join you in your holy place. Please come for me and take me home.

Lord, let my departure from this world make your name known and glorified throughout the world and in all ages. Let those who will come or hear my departure rejoice and glorify your name because I will not be dead but I shall have gone home. In just the same way that you gave back life to many when Jesus was resurrected, it is my humble prayer that during those seven days may the world receive the fire of the Holy Ghost. May everything that is abomination be consumed by the fire of the Holy Ghost. Let everyone receive it and talk in tongues without discriminating by race, colour, nationality, religion, or in any way whatsoever. Let the Devil and his followers be powerless and bow before you and acknowledge that Jesus is the Lord. May the world receive peace and salvation that comes from your throne, Lord, on that day.

Lord, maybe by the time my soul separates from my body I will be unconscious and not understand what is about to happen. Lord, it is my sincere prayer that you will remember this prayer I am praying today. Write it in the Book of Remembrance. Lord, it is my prayer that you will give me back my senses if I will have lost them when that time comes. It is my prayer not to leave this world through pain or suffering of any kind. I do not need to suffer to come home. My door is open for you and ready to come home at any time it is convenient for you. But let your will be done.

PART II

CHAPTER 15

MAN IS A COMPLICATED CREATURE

In Genesis 1:31, God looked at everything He created, and He was very pleased. In Genesis 4:7, when the Lord God created the universe, there were no plants on the earth and no seeds had sprouted, because he had not sent any rain, and there was no one to cultivate the land; but water would come up from beneath the surface and water the ground. Then the Lord God took some soil from the ground and formed a man out of it; He breathed life-giving breath into his nostrils and the man began to live. The Lord God planted a Garden of Eden, in the East, and there he put the man he had formed. He made all kinds of beautiful trees, which produced good fruit. In the middle of the garden stood the tree that gives life and the tree that gives knowledge of what is good and what is bad. In Genesis 2:15–16, then the Lord God placed the man in the Garden of Eden so that he might cultivate it and guard it. He said to him, *"You may eat the fruit of any tree in the garden, except the tree that gives knowledge of what is good and what is bad. You must not eat the fruit of that tree; if you do, you will die the same day."*

God was right. Before Adam was formed from the soil, he was not known by God. After committing sin, Adam was chased from the Garden of Eden and forgotten in the eyes of God. This means that he died the same day because God withdrew his presence from the world.

In Genesis 3:22–24, the Lord God said, *"Now the man has become like one of us and has knowledge of what is good and what is bad. He must not be allowed to eat the fruit from the tree of life, and live forever."* So the Lord God sent him out of the Garden of Eden and made him cultivate the soil from which he had been formed. Then, at the east side of the garden, he put living creatures and a flaming sword, which turned in all directions. This was to keep anyone from coming near the tree of life.

In Genesis 8:20–22, Noah built an altar to the Lord; he took one of each kind of animal and burnt them whole as a sacrifice on the altar. The odor of the sacrifice pleased the Lord, and he said to himself, *"Never again will I put the earth under a curse because of what man does; I know that from the time he is young, his thoughts are evil. Never again will I destroy all living beings, as I have done this time. As long as the world exists, there will be a time for planting and a time for harvest. There will always be cold and heat, summer and winter, day and night."*

In Genesis 11:5–9, the Lord came down to see the city and the tower, which those men had built, and he said, *"Now then, these are all one people and they speak one language; this is just the beginning of what they are going to do. Soon they will be able to do anything they want. Let us go down and mix up their language so that they will not understand one another."* So the Lord scattered them all over the earth, and they stopped building the city. The city was called Babel, because there the Lord mixed up the language of all the people, and from there he scattered them all over the earth.

In Genesis 18:20–21, the Lord God said to Abraham, "*There are terrible accusations against Sodom and Gomorrah, and their sin is very great. I must go down to find out whether or not the accusations I have heard are true.*"

In Genesis 22:1–2: Sometime later God tested Abraham; he called to him, "*Abraham!*" And Abraham answered, "*Yes, here I am!*" "*Take your son,*" God said, "*your only son, Isaac, whom you love so much, and go to the land of Moriah. There on a mountain that I will show you, offer him as a sacrifice to me.*" Abraham did as he was commanded. In Genesis 22:10–12, Abraham picked up the knife to kill his son, Isaac. But the angel of the Lord called to him from heaven, "*Abraham, Abraham!*" He answered, "*Yes, here I am.*" "*Do not hurt the boy or do anything to him,*" the angel said. "*Now I know that you fear God, because you have not kept back your only son from him.*". God provided a lamb and blessed Abraham.

In Exodus 15:25–26: "There the Lord gave them laws to live by, and there he also tested them. He said, "*If you will obey me completely by doing what I consider right and by keeping my commands, I will not punish you with any of the diseases that I brought on Egypt. I am the Lord, the one who heals you.*"

In Exodus 20:20, Moses replied, "*Do not be afraid; God has only come to test you and make you keep on fearing him, so that you will not sin.*" But the people continued to stand a long way off, and only Moses went near the dark cloud where God was.

In Numbers 14:11–12, the Lord said to Moses, "*How much longer will these people reject me? How much longer will they refuse to trust in me, even though I have performed so many miracles among them? I will send an epidemic and destroy them, but I will make you the father of a nation that is larger and more powerful than they are!"*

In Numbers 2:18, the Israelites left mount Hor by the road that leads to the Gulf of Aqaba, in order to go around the territory of Edom. But on the way, the people lost their patience and spoke against God and Moses. They complained, *"Why did you bring us out of Egypt to die in this desert, where there is no food or water? We cannot stand any more of this miserable food!"* Then the Lord sent poisonous snakes among the people, and many Israelites were bitten and died. The people came to Moses and said, *"We sinned when we spoke against the Lord and against you. Now pray to the Lord to take these snakes away."* So Moses prayed for the people. Then the Lord told Moses to make a metal snake and put it on a pole, so that anyone who was bitten could look at it and be healed.

In Deuteronomy. 11:26–28: *"Today I am giving you the choice between a blessing and a curse; a blessing if you obey the commands of the Lord your God that I am giving you today but a curse if you disobey these commands and turn away to worship other gods that you have never worshiped before . . . "*

In 1 Samuel 15:10–11: The Lord said to Samuel, *"I am sorry that I made Saul king; he has turned away from me and disobeyed my commands."* Samuel was angry, and all night long he pleaded with the Lord.

It is hard to understand man because something else that God had no intention to create was created after eating the fruit of the tree that gives knowledge of what is good and what is bad. Man became a complicated creature and that is why we suffer, because we need to prove to God that we can be faithful and trusted once more. Our first parent chose to follow or listen to a stranger, the Devil. He ignored the instructions that he was given by God, despite being given everything by his creator. The woman (Eve) ignored instructions she was given by her husband (Adam) and Adam ignored instructions given to him by God. Therefore, Eve adored the Devil, and Adam adored his wife (Eve).

CHAPTER 16

SWEARING AN OATH

It is wrong to make promises that we do not know we will be able to keep. God hates anyone who makes promises without keeping them, no matter what. That is why God discourages mortal man from making promises, because our failure to fulfill them will result in curses.

Only God is worthy to make covenants/promises, because no matter what comes our way, He will make His promises come true. In Genesis 15:1–18, God said to Abraham to bring Him a cow, a goat, a ram, each of them three years old, a dove and a pigeon, and to cut them in half, except the birds. When the sun set and it was dark, a smoking firepot and a flaming torch suddenly appeared and was passed between the pieces of the animals. Then the Lord God made a covenant with Abraham.

God could not allow Abraham to pass between the pieces of the animal because he was not supposed to make any promises to God. All that God wanted from Abraham was trust and obedience. God made all the promises to mankind and has never allowed any man to make promises.

Therefore, it is wrong for anyone to stand before the Lord and congregation to make a covenant with his wife or her husband. It would be better if the church leaders could change those binding marriage promises, because they lead to sins that make God angry. Instead, it should be, "God (not I), help me to take so and so. Help me to love him/her in times of need, sickness, and everything." In this way, you are not making promises to one another but asking God to commit you to loving your spouse. God will not let you fail, because you did not make your own promise. God is faithful and will remain faithful to your marriage so long as you recognize His presence in your midst. This will allow you to remain submissive to God because you will be following His will. Making your own promises means that sometimes you will be against God's will, trying to stand on your own promises. In that case, you will adore your spouse more than God, and as a result, you will have broken the first commandment of God.

Jesus said that whoever loves his/her parent, child, or spouse more than he/she loves God is not worthy to receive the kingdom of God. Involve God in everything that you do. Hold fast in the promises of God, but do not stand in your own promises. If you make a promise, then make sure you fulfill it no matter what comes your way, no exceptions or excuses.

In Psalms 15:1–5, one of the things that God requires is a person who always does what he promises, no matter how much it may cost. The reason why we are not supposed to make promises is because the Devil lays traps through them.

Homes are built on the foundation of wisdom and understanding. Where there is knowledge, the rooms are furnished with valuable, beautiful things. The knowledge and wisdom comes from God.

It is wrong to ask anyone to make promises because you are helping the Devil to lay traps on you. We should only trust and obey our God and leave promises to Him. Commitment is a law, but we are bound with love, because law results in death, but love gives live.

In the book of Acts 5:1–11, Ananias and his wife Sapphira promised to sell the property that belonged to them and give all the money to the Lord. They were not forced but did it voluntarily. After selling the property, they became greedy and decided to keep part of the money for themselves. Peter, the disciple of Jesus, asked him, "Before you sold the property, it belonged to you, and after you sold it, the money was yours. Why then did you lie to God?" As soon as Ananias heard those words, he fell down and died. His wife came and testified the same thing. Both of them were buried the same day. Why did they die? They died because they failed to keep their promise. If they had sold their property and quietly taken a part to God, then God could have blessed them in a mighty way. But now they could no longer enjoy their property. Maybe their names were removed from the book of life because of their false promises.

It is wrong to promise God anything. You may end up inheriting curses from God instead of blessings. People, especially Christians, disgust God in many ways. Many Christians think that God cannot bless them. They begin to tell God, "If you bless me with this, I will give you that in return." Unfortunately, the Devil is not asleep. At the time you are receiving your blessings—such as a job or salary increase—more problems are awaiting you. You divide your money and find that it is not enough to cater to your needs, and maybe you had promised God 10% or maybe half of your salary. Now, at this time, you give your problems first priority, and the promise you made with your God second priority. In fact, you end up telling him that he will understand. You know what? God is just and very understanding. He will understand that you do not deserve his blessings. Who has cursed you? Not God, but you told him to understand and give you what you deserve.

The best promise you can ever make to God that pleases Him is this: "God, if you bless me, I will give glory and honor to you. I will give thanks to you and praise your holy name." Surely no matter what comes, you cannot fail to say, "Thank you, God, may your name be glorified. You are worthy, God, to be praised and worshipped by all your creation." You will remain righteous throughout your life. Why bribe God for blessings? God is a loving and kind Father.

Judicial Systems

I do respect judicial systems of all kinds because of the hard work they do to separate the truth from the lies, trying to be fair and just. They need wisdom and guidance from God.

But it is wrong for any judicial system to use any Holy Book, whether a Bible, Koran, or other holy book, for people to swear by or take an oath that they are going to tell the truth to the court. In the Bible, in the book of Deuteronomy 4:15–24, God warned against idolatry. Holy books contain the word of God but do not represent God Himself. Therefore, using a holy book to prove that one is telling the truth is not only forcing one to worship an idol but also forcing one to use the name of God in vain. Whoever holds a Bible in court and takes an oath of telling the truth breaks the first three commandments of God, no matter whether the person is guilty or innocent. This is what God said about those who fail to keep the first three commandments: "*I am the Lord your God, and I tolerate no rivals. I bring punishment on those who hate me and on their descendants down to the third and fourth generation. But I show my love to thousands of generations of those who love me and obey my laws."* The only way to hate God is by failing to keep the first three commandments.

If the court feels that they want to include God, it is very much okay because the judges need wisdom and the knowledge that comes from God in order to be fair and just in their verdicts. Instead, the judicial systems should use a phrase like, "God, I stand in your presence and before the judge in order to testify to the truth that is in my heart. Help me, God, to tell the truth and nothing but the whole truth." Give God the respect that He deserves and His word, too. God prohibits anyone from swearing. The truth is in one's heart. How would you feel if your child kept on swearing with your name to justify that he or she is telling the truth?

It is wrong for a judge to be prejudiced. If the judge pronounces a guilty person innocent, he/she will be cursed and hated by everyone. However, judges who punish the guilt will be prosperous and enjoy a good reputation.

Blessed is the nation that keeps and obeys God's law. A nation without God's guidance is a nation without order.

CHAPTER 17

LEADERSHIP

I respect political leaders and other leaders because I believe leadership comes from God.

Politicians are physical leaders, while religious leaders are spiritual leaders. Those who fear God and obey His command must respect and submit to any authority. You cannot criticize your leaders and then kneel down to pray for them. The moment you criticize them, you have passed judgment, and God will do according to your heart's desire: Condemnation. If you want to be a good spiritual leader, support your leaders with prayers because God will hear your prayers. When you say yes, it will be yes to God ,because whatever you have bound in this world shall be bound in heaven, and whatever you set free in this world shall be set free indeed according to the gospel of Jesus. Why waste your time talking too much instead of using the best tool for airing your grievances to the king of kings, which is through prayer.

Leaders must not be ignorant of the fact that they are God's vessels. God anoints them from heaven to lead His people in the righteous and prosperous way. They are called to be servants of people or shepherds. They are not called to oppress people but to help them to stay focused. It is not possible to control more than two people, but God has given them favor, power, and authority to lead. Adam and Eve were two in the Garden of Eden, yet they decided to rebel against God. What about the millions of people that you do not even know, yet you claim that you control them? It is not possible. But through God's grace, it is possible. Therefore, respect your people, knowing that they are children of God and that their cries will surely be heard in heaven.

God made you leaders so that you could feed the poor, rescue those who are oppressed, and be the voice of the orphans and widows in the community. Most leaders fail because they walk their own way out of pride. Remember there are three things God hates and cannot tolerate from anyone—*a proud look, hands that kill innocent people, and a man who stirs up trouble among friends.* Those are the three things that make God bring down a leader. He has the power to lift one from dust to a king and from a king to dust. Remember the story of Nebuchadnezzar: God gave him the power and authority to punish God's people. After conquering all the neighboring tribes, he uplifted his name instead of uplifting the name of Jehovah God. God did not spare him and instead sent him to the forest to eat grass for seven years. After seven years, God remembered him and restored him back to the throne; he thereafter worshipped and glorified the Most High God. This story is in the book of the Old Testament.

The Lord God controls the mind of a king as easily as he directs the course of a stream. You may think that everything you do is right because you are a leader and you have power and authority, but remember that the Most High God will judge your motives. You were anointed to represent God, to lead His children home safely. Your primary goal is to feed the children, not to grab or steal or loot from them, but to heal their hearts by giving them hope and encouragement—not to break their hearts by enslaving them, but to reconcile them and not separate the children of God.

Politicians are God's vessels. Yet, due to ignorance, they are used by the Devil to kill, steal, and destroy. Their power and authority must be used for the glory of God, not for personal interest or gain.

We are all equal in the eyes of the Lord. No one is greater than any other. We came into this world with nothing, and we will carry nothing from it. Power, authority, and wealth do not make us greater in the eyes of God. In fact, God has blessed us with everything that we have. It is not through our effort, power, or wisdom. It is only that we are privileged to be leaders made by the almighty God. The Lord gives and can take away.

Whatever we do with our power and authority should be for the glory of God. God hates the killing and suffering of innocent people. He always hears the cries of women and children, no matter what motive we think we have. We can give all the excuses we want, but God will hear the cries of innocent people. No one has the right to take away the life of another person. If you kill by the sword, then you die by the sword. It does not matter what religion you belong to—those are the basic principles of life. Peace does not come by the sword but by sweet and kind words. Swords kill; good, sweet and kind words heal. If you do wrong or misuse power, you cannot escape punishment from God. God is watching you from His Holy City.

My brothers and sisters do not lean on spiritual leaders because they are also human, like you. Seek guidance from God, and be careful with some of those spiritual leaders. Some are being used by the Devil to fulfill his dreams. When God elevates one spiritual leader, the Devil elevates ten. Raise up, people of all nations, support your leaders with prayers and refuse to be misled. Remember that when God brings disaster or punishment to those leaders, it will strike you first.

When a country invades another country, we blame politicians, but when natural calamities occur, we blame spiritual leaders. It is the responsibility of any spiritual leader to protect their flock or people from natural calamities. Natural calamities occur because God wants to glorify himself, or because it is a punishment from God, or because the Devil wants to destroy human beings. For us to experience the power of God and in return to be able to praise and glorify his mighty name, God allows calamities to occur so that if we sincerely call upon His name, He can save us by performing miracles. Sometimes we are in trouble or fall sick—not because God wants us to die but so that He can perform miracles. He is only waiting for us to call upon His name, and then everything calms down. Sometimes God becomes furious with our evil ways and intends to punish us. If we repent our sins and sincerely call upon His name, He will forgive us and save us.

When the Devil is ready to destroy us, God will protect us. The Devil can do no harm to those who trust and obey the Most High God. It is the responsibility of the spiritual leaders to teach their people how to pray and watch out. Sometimes we need to praise and worship God to receive miracles, sometimes we need to humble ourselves and repent our sins to be saved, and other times we need to rebuke and cast out the Devil and the power of darkness. Material blessings are useless when danger comes, but spiritual blessings become our shield and weapon to protect us.

God does not require a majority in order to save or heal a nation. He only needs one person who is faithful to Him. It is not the will of God to destroy human beings, but sometimes we destroy ourselves due to lack of knowledge. Through one man (Adam) we run short of God's glory, and through one man (Jesus) we are restored to His glory. Our spiritual leaders are blind. Our people who believe in God are blind, too. When I see the storms and floods killing innocent people, I feel pain deep within my heart. Do those people really deserve to die? Where is our God, who we claim is our Father? Does it mean He can only bless us with riches but cannot protect us from natural disasters? Does God really exist and love us? Is He merciful to us?

The answer is that God loves the world and cares for us. He has given us wisdom to choose what is good and bad. It is our responsibility to know what we need and ask for it. This world belongs to us, and we have the power and authority to protect it. Everything that God created on earth was put under man's feet. The winds, the water, and the current in the oceans can obey our commands. We need to speak a word and divert their directions. All that we need to do is to do according to God's will. We need to stand in the promises of God. The spiritual leaders need to teach people how to stay in the house of the Lord. We cannot stay without God because of the danger that is ahead of us. We all need God. We need to turn back to God by repenting our sins as individuals and as a nation to gain God's favor; otherwise, we are going to perish.

God is ready to teach us His way. He will teach us how to pray and when to do so because He will be revealing what is ahead of us before it happens. We will not pray blindly and then perish while still fasting and praying. We need to trust and obey Him. Spiritual leaders must trust and believe there is a God first, before they teach us. They need to establish a good relationship with God and walk in His grace every day. They should stop being signboards that only point to Holy City when they have an agenda, or they will never be there. The spiritual leaders are responsible for the sins of those people, who become victims of those natural calamities and die. It's their responsibility to protect people, and that is why they are called shepherds. Our souls are entrusted to their hands, and they should protect us from danger. The spiritual leaders have failed, but every one of us has failed because all of us are equal in the eyes of the Lord. One of us can save the whole world if that one person has established a good relationship with God.

When God became angry with the children of Israel, Moses as a good shepherd stood in the gap between God and them by interceding and pleading with God to forgive them. Abraham stood in the gap between God and Lot, his nephew. We need to remember that we are called to intercede for our people to God. We need to carry their burden and ask God to forgive them through us. We cannot walk blindly waiting to count losses. We are alive, but not walking corpses or dead bodies.

But because He is a loving God, He will always show us what is ahead of us.

My advice to you leaders is that you must learn how to trust in the Most High God with all your heart. Never rely on what you think you know. Remember God in everything you do, and He will show you the right way to lead His children. Never let yourself think that you are wiser than you are; simply obey God, the creator of the universe, and refuse to do wrong. Whether you are a politician or a spiritual leader, you must have a human heart. Be a good shepherd because God is watching you. It is only through God's favor that you became a leader, not because of your ability, wealth, or goodness. It is wrong to control people without their will or consent. It is a satanic and demonic way of tormenting people with fear. God's way is by wining people's hearts through love, kindness, friendship and sweet words. Be humble and you will not only reign on earth but also in the New Jerusalem, the Holy City, together with Jesus, the king of kings.

CHAPTER 18

AMAZING VISION ABOUT CHURCHES

One night, the spirit of God took control of me, and I was taken high into the sky. There was someone next to me whom I could not recognize, but I could feel the presence and holiness of God. At the place where I was, I could see everything in the world. I saw that about 85% of the big, decorated buildings that had once been covered with the glory and beauty of God had now become ugly, with a dirty rug as a flag. The rest were white everywhere (as if they had been covered with snow) and had a floating flag (the flag was red and a luminous green). They looked very beautiful.

I became curious about those buildings and wanted to know more. I asked the gentleman who was next to me to explain more about those buildings. He looked at me and said, "Charles, those are churches," and he kept quiet. Then I asked, "Sir, why do most of those churches look ugly?" He looked straight into my eyes, smiled, and then said to me, "Charles, Jesus shed his blood as the price of salvation to mankind. He brought the salvation and peace that the Devil had stolen from mankind. Red represents salvation, the redemption through blood, and the luminous green represents peace. The buildings with flags are the true churches of God because the righteous and faithful people go to those buildings to praise and worship God. They are truly the children of God. The dirty rug is the flag of the Devil. A church can either have a dirty rug or a flag, but not both. The white paint represents the holiness of God while many colors represent the presence of confusion, the kingdom of darkness. Those who go to those buildings that have rugs claim to be worshipping God, but their hearts seek God for things other than salvation. Wait and see what is going to happen."

Then I saw people converging on those buildings in small groups because it was on a Sunday morning. What surprised me was that many people came to those buildings with rugs while few went to the buildings with the flag of Jesus. After a while, the buildings with rugs were turned into marketplaces of all kinds. It was noisy, and there was a lot of confusion. Most of the people looked naked, and those who were not naked were not decently dressed. There was music that sounded like loud noise and people were dancing as if they were in a pub. This means there was confusion because people were moving in different directions. I was really ashamed and said nothing, but tried to close my eyes.

Then I looked to the few buildings with flags, and I saw a few people converging on the buildings. They were covered with rings of light. When they sang, they were singing with the same voice, moving in the same direction, without confusion. Then I saw heaven open, and the angels were ascending and descending to those buildings with flags. The buildings that had held few people at first were now overcrowded, even in the compound outside. I could hardly differentiate between a human and an angel. They all looked the same.

I was disturbed and asked the gentleman with me to help me understand more about what was happening. He said to me, "Charles, those people who are attending the buildings with flags are the true worshippers of God. They are poor in their hearts, and all that they need is to seek God. They have left everything behind and followed God with one purpose, salvation. Their hearts' desire is to inherit the kingdom of

God by winning God's heart. They have cleansed their garments in the blood of Jesus and have become true ambassadors of heaven on earth, though none of them are recognized or noticed on earth. But those who attend the buildings with rugs are preoccupied with many things. Their hearts have no room for God. They are seeking God for their businesses to be smooth, but they have no vision of salvation. Their hearts are rich with earthly material things, and they have no hunger or thirst for the word of God because they do not believe that one day they will die. In fact, if you give them a choice, either to die and be with God or to live forever, they will choose to live forever. Anyone who loves God will desire to be with God, but those who love the world will desire to live forever. The heart is always where the treasure is."

Then the gentleman with me took me to another place and revealed to me more secrets regarding those buildings.

Secrets Behind Miracles

I was taken to another place where I could see the whole world, including the sea. The gentleman said to me, "Charles, this is what happened to those buildings with rugs." I saw a king ascending from the sea, wearing a crown like Jesus, with a white robe. Beside him, there were creatures that looked like angels. He ascended to the sky and seemed to be above the mainland. I heard him declaring himself to be Jesus, but I doubted him. Then he opened his mouth and many white objects, like eggs or bubbles, came out and fell on the ground. After a while, he made the rain fall from the sky, and this dissolved those eggs, and the plants absorbed the water with eggs. Those eggs were transferred to the human body through plants or the animals that ate the plants. In the human system, the eggs were formed from the liquid, hatched, and then grown into the human body. Those people had direct communication with the king, who rose from the sea.

Then I heard the same king boasting, saying, "Now we have control over human beings. We are going to keep human beings very busy by creating problems and providing solutions at the same time. When humans have no peace and are overcome with problems, they will be willing to come to us for solutions. We are going to perform miracles. There is no miracle that will ever satisfy human beings because their problems will always be greater than the miracles we provide. Their prayers will never go beyond our kingdom because we will answer their prayers immediately, and therefore they will have no time to think or seek the real God or follow the teachings of the real Jesus Christ. Human beings will think that God is close to them, and that is why they are receiving miracles. They will convince themselves that if God is not with us, why then is He performing miracles for us? They will receive everything that they may ask for as proof that God has heard their prayers. In this case, they will forget the important miracle from God, which is salvation. They will be too busy asking for miracles and forget to ask for forgiveness of their sins. They will have no time to cleanse themselves. This is the only way we can confuse the world."

Then the gentleman with me pulled a curtain, and what I saw was shocking. I saw powerful spiritual leaders, whom I knew were performing miracles in the name of the impersonated Jesus. They had a large number of followers and were preaching about the kingdom of God, but what amazed me was that they were holding the Bible upside down, but none of their followers noticed. In the pulpit, they were changing into different funny, ugly creatures, such as snakes, pigs, and dogs. Fire poured through their mouths and nostrils. But I saw the multitudes that believed in those spiritual leaders, and I pitied them because they were lost.

I asked the gentleman with me whether those spiritual leaders were aware of what they were doing. He said to me, "Charles, most of them do not know where they get the power and authority, because they may not agree. They believe that they are serving the Most High God. You cannot convince them that they are misleading God's people and being used by the Devil that has impersonated Jesus. When God raises one servant, the Devil raises a hundred. Only those with the spirit of discernment will recognize them. This is the time when the anti-Christ is active. The prophecy has come to pass. Many will perform miracles to mislead people, but his flock knows him. Happy are those who seek God with a clean heart for forgiveness of sins because they will not fall into the Devil's trap. That is how those buildings with rugs came into existence. Go and tell them to change those houses into houses of prayer and not into a marketplace."

"People believe that God will be pleased and respect expensive buildings. God's spirit does not reside in buildings but in human hearts. Your hearts are the true buildings for the Most High God, not the expensive buildings. During the day of the judgment, no stone will be lying on top of the other, but the true church, the human heart, will remain forever. Those buildings can be valuable if the people in them are true worshippers of God. Where the presence of God is, anything nearby is made holy."

I do believe in miracles because God performed miracles through Moses, the prophets, and Jesus. It is through miracles that we believe that God exists. But our relationship with God is not built on those miracles. Our faith is built on the love and grace of God. Our hope and trust is built on the rock, Jesus Christ. We all have to receive the greatest miracle of all, the forgiveness of sins. God loved us before we loved him and gave us the most precious miracle, salvation. Therefore, with or without other miracles we are spiritually satisfied because we have hope for life after death. Those who have no hope are spiritually dead. Every minute you are receiving the miracle of life—the air you breathe, the circulation of blood in your body, the beating of your heart, all of it. Give thanks and glory to God for these things.

Matthew 16:1–4: *Some Pharisees and Sadducees who came to Jesus wanted to trap him, so they asked him to perform a miracle for them, to show that God approved of him. But Jesus answered, "When the sun is setting, you say, 'we are going to have fine weather, because the sky is red.' And early in the morning you say, 'It is going to rain, because the sky is red and dark.' You can predict the weather by looking at the sky, but you cannot interpret the signs concerning these times! How evil and godless are the people of this day! You ask me for a miracle? No! The only miracle you will be given is the miracle of Jonah." So he left them and went away.* Jonah was swallowed by a fish for three days and in the same way Jesus was to be swallowed by the ground for three days. The resurrection of Jesus Christ on the third day was the greatest miracle, the miracle of salvation. No resurrection, no salvation. So what does this mean for those who claim greater miracles than this? Surely they read their Bibles upside down.

Do not be ignorant about the time. Remember when Moses, with his brother, was sent to pharaoh for the first time? They performed miracles, but the pharaoh was not surprised because his sorcerers could perform the same miracle. Moses laid down a stick and turned it to a snake. The sorcerer did the same. The only difference was that Moses' snake overcame the other snakes and swallowed them all.

There is evidence in the Bible in the book of Revelation 13. " It says the John saw the beast coming up out of the sea…. the dragon gave the beast his own power, his throne and vast authority…the whole earth was amazed and followed the beast. Everyone worshipped the dragon because he had given his authority to the beast. They worshipped the beast also, 'who is like the beast? Who can fight against it?'

'It began to curse God, His name, the place where He lives, and all those live in heaven. It was allowed to defeat them, and it was given authority over every tribe, nation, language and race. All people living on earth will worship it, except those whose names were written before the creation of the world in the book of the living which belongs to the Lamb that was killed, Jesus the Christ."

The prophecy in the book of Revelation 13:10 said that whoever is meant to be captured will surely be captured; whoever is meant to be killed by the sword will surely be killed by the sword. This prophecy calls for endurance and faith on the part of God's people.

False Prophets

Before the angel of God left, he whispered to me about the prophecies of both Ezekiel and Jeremiah in connection to those false prophets. Later, after I woke up, I read those two books, and they made a lot of sense.

Prophet Ezekiel's Message

Do the prophets make up their own prophecies? In the Bible, the book of Ezekiel 13, God warned against false prophets. This is what God had to say through the prophet Ezekiel. *"These foolish prophets are doomed! They provide their own inspiration and invent their own visions. Christians of today, your prophets are as useless as foxes living among the ruins of the city. They do not guard the places where the walls have crumbled, nor do they build the walls, and so the churches cannot be defended when war comes on the day of the Lord. Their visions are false, and their predictions are lies. They claim that they are speaking my message, but I have not sent them. Yet they expect their words to come true! I tell them: Those visions you see are false, and the predictions you make are lies. You say that they are my words, but I have not spoken to you!*

"Your words are false, and visions are lies. I am against you. I am about to punish you prophets who have false visions and make misleading predictions. You will not be there when my people gather to make decisions; your names will not be included in the list of the Heir or citizens of the Holy Place of God; you will never return to your land.

"The prophets mislead my people by saying that all is well. All is certainly not well! My people have put up a wall of loose stones, and then the prophets have come and covered it with whitewash. Tell the prophets that their wall is going to fall down. I will send a pouring rain. Hailstones will fall on it, and a strong wind will blow against it. The wall will collapse, and everyone will ask you what good the whitewash did.

"You are doomed! You sew magic wristbands for everyone and make magic scarves for everyone to wear on their heads, so that you can have power over my people's lives. You want to possess the power of life and death over my people and to use it for your own benefit. You dishonor me in front of my people in order to get a few handfuls of barley and a few pieces of bread. You kill people who do not deserve to die, and you keep people alive who do

not deserve to live because you benefit from them. You tell lies to my people, and they believe you.

"I hate the wristbands that you use in your attempt to control life and death. I will rip them off your arms and set free the people that you were controlling. I will rip off your scarves and let my people escape from your power once and for all.

"By your lies you discourage good people, whom I do not wish to hurt. You prevent evil people from giving up evil and saving their lives. So now your false visions and misleading predictions are over. I am rescuing my people from your power.

"In my anger I will send a strong wind, pouring rain, and hailstones to destroy the wall. I intend to break down the wall they whitewashed, to shatter it, and to leave the foundation stones bare. It will collapse and kill you all.

"The wall and those who covered it with whitewash will feel the force of my anger. Then I will tell you that the wall is gone and so are those who whitewashed it—those prophets who assured my people that all is well, when it is not well! Then you will know that I am the Lord."

Prophet Jeremiah's Message

The land is full of people who are unfaithful to the Lord; they live wicked lives and misuse their power. Because of the Lord's curse, the land mourns and the pastures are dry. This is what the Lord said through the prophet Jeremiah:

"The prophets and priests are godless; I have caught them doing evil in the Holy Places of God, in the altar itself. The paths they follow will be slippery and dark; I will make them stumble and fall. I am going to bring disaster on them; the time of their punishment is coming.

"I have seen the sin of the prophets and priests; they have led my people astray. They commit adultery and tell lies; they help people to do wrong, so that no one stops doing what is evil. To me, they are all as bad as the people of Sodom and Gomorrah. I will give them bitter plants to eat and poison to drink, because they have spread ungodliness throughout the land.

"Tell my people not to listen to what those false prophets say; they are filling you with false hopes. They tell you what they have imagined and not what I have said. To the people who refuse to listen to what I have said, they keep saying that all will go well with them. And they tell everyone who is stubborn that disaster will never touch him."

"None of these false prophets has ever known my secret thoughts. None of them have ever heard or understood my message, or ever listened or paid attention to what I said. My anger is a storm, a furious wind that will rage overhead of the wicked, and it will not end until I have done everything I intend to do. In days to come my people will understand this clearly.

"I did not send these prophets, but even so they went. I did not give them my message, but still they spoke in my name. If they had known my secret thoughts, then they could have proclaimed my message to my people and could have made them give up the evil lives they live and the wicked things they do.

"I am a God who is everywhere and not in one place only. No one can hide where I cannot see him. Do you know that I am everywhere in heaven and on earth? I know what those prophets have said who speak lies in my name and claim that I have given them my messages in their dreams. How much longer will those prophets mislead my people with the lies they have *invented? They think that the dreams they tell will make my people forget me. The prophet who has had a dream should say it is only a dream, but the prophet who has heard my message should proclaim that message faithfully. What good is straw compared with wheat? My message is like a fire, and like a hammer that breaks rocks in pieces. I am against those prophets who take each other's words and proclaim them as my message. I am also against those prophets who speak their own words and claim they came from me. Listen to what I, the Lord, say! I am against the prophets who tell their dreams that are full of lies. They tell these dreams and lead my people astray with their lies and their boasting.*

"I did not send them or order them to go, and they are of no help at all to my people, I, the Lord, have spoken."

CHAPTER 19

LIVING A DOUBLE LIFE

The majority of Christians are believers, but they do not know what they believe in. They are emotional and believe the preachers because the preachers are able to address their needs, and since the preachers are promising solutions, they get carried away. Others are there to exploit the opportunity of living a better life.

In simple words, some preachers are bribing people to come for salvation. Those preachers are blinded by the Devil. They promise material things as a reward. This is wrong. Salvation is free from God. None of us are worthy to receive it, but through God's grace it is free. This is a powerful weapon of the Devil and a big trap that he has laid down, especially for Christians who are called by Jesus' name. The majority of Christians have sought salvation not because they want to be forgiven of their sins but because they are aiming to receive wealth and a better life. Be aware of such preachers and prophets, for they speak sweet words like honey, full of promises, but they speak rarely about the repentant, the kingdom of God. They will tell you how much they have acquired physically but less about the kingdom of God. Every word they speak needs to be paid for because they are always stretching their hands out to receive something. They tell you to trust in God for blessings or to give you more, but they trust in you to provide them with their needs. They tell you to sow the seeds of love so that you will be blessed. They give testimonies of how much they receive after giving and how much you can give to receive. They trade with the name of the living God. They want to build the best building in the world for fame while the true church of Christ is built with rejects, rags, and mud in the hearts of the congregation. They want their buildings to have golden streets, but the true house of the Lord, spiritually, is full of rats and cockroaches. They use business slogans in their advertisements instead of the true word of God that builds and heals the nation. To them, some miracles are greater than others. They speak as if they are the ones who decide which miracle is greater.

My dear friend, the Bible tells us that God so loved the world that He gave his only begotten son, for whosoever believes in Him shall not perish but have eternal life. The world gave nothing to God to receive salvation. God is not a beggar, or poor. He is not desperate to offer salvation to anyone. He does not need people who are bribed, but He is ready to offer salvation to those who are in need of salvation.

Being blessed with salvation is one thing, and being blessed with wealth is another thing altogether. The choice is yours. God is ready to bless those who are poor in heart. You do not have to give to be blessed by God. In fact, God blesses His people while they are sleeping, not when they are awake. Giving should not be perceived as lending to God, because God is the creator of everything and therefore we owe Him everything—He owes us nothing. Being a blessing to others will increase your blessings because God will trust you by blessing others through you. This means that you will become like a water pipe that draws water from one source to carry it to many destinations.

The act of giving should be treated as you would a king who owns everything. A king's son enjoyed his father's wealth and nobody questioned him. But one day the son decided to buy his father a very simple gift for a certain occasion. The father who was king, would receive that gift with great honor and would increase the son's blessings. But what if the son gave the gift expecting to receive a hundred fold in return? This would mean that if the son told the father that a gift was a debt, the father would not accept it. And imagine if every day the son kept on reminding the father that he owed him a hundred- fold of the gift he had received from him. His father would not be happy. In a very real sense, this would betray their trust and would cause the father to reduce his blessings to the son. A wise son would approach his father wisely to gain favor.

Does God Expect a Miracle?

Miracles are not a good measure of salvation or of the good relationship between man and God. In fact, in Deuteronomy 13:1–4 it states: *"A prophet or an interpreter of dreams may promise a miracle or a wonder in order to lead you to worship and serve gods that you have not worshipped before. Even if what he promises comes true, do not pay any attention to him. The Lord your God is using him to test you, to see if you love the Lord with all your heart..."* And in Revelation 16:13–14: *"...then I saw three unclean spirits that looked like frogs. They were coming out of the mouth of the dragon, the mouth of the beast, and the mouth of the false prophet. They are the spirits of demons that perform miracles. These three spirits go out to all the kings of the world, to bring them together for the battle on the great Day of Almighty God."* Revelation 13:13–14: *"...this second beast performed great miracles; it made fire come down out of heaven to earth in the sight of everyone. And it deceived all the people living on earth by means of the miracles, which it was allowed to perform in the presence of the first beast."*

In his teaching, in the book of Matthew 16:24–26: "… Jesus said: *If anyone wants to go with me, he must forget self, carry his cross, and follow me. For whoever wants to save his own life will lose it; but whoever loses his life for his sake will find it. Will a person gain anything if he wins the whole world but loses his life? Of course not! There is nothing he can give to regain his life.*" He also said that whoever wants to follow him must follow his footsteps and drink of his cup. This means that one must be ready to go through temptations and suffering.

In Luke 6:22–26, Jesus looked at his disciples and said, "*Happy are you when people hate you, reject you, insult you, and say that you are evil, all because of the son of man. Be glad when that happens, and dance for joy, because a great reward is kept for you in heaven. For their ancestors did the very same things to the prophets. But how terrible for you who are rich now; you have had your easy life. How terrible for you who are full now; you will go hungry. How terrible for you who laugh now; you will mourn and weep. How terrible when all people speak well of you; their ancestors said the very same things about the false prophets.*

In Luke 12:15, Jesus warned against greediness: "*Watch out and guard yourselves from every kind of greed; because a person's true life is not made up of the things he owns, no matter how rich he may be.*" And in Luke 21:34-36: "*Be on your guard! Do not let yourselves become occupied with too much feasting and drinking and with the worries of this life, or that day may suddenly catch you like a trap. For it will come upon all people everywhere on earth. Be on the alert and pray always that you will have the strength to go safely through all those things that will happen and to stand before the son of man.*"

In John 4:13–14, Jesus said, "*Whoever drinks this water will be thirsty again. But whoever drinks the water that I will give him will never thirst again."* In John 7:37: *"...whoever is thirsty should come to me and drink . . . whoever believes in me, streams of life-giving water will pour out from his heart."* In John 6:27: *"Do not work for food that goes bad; instead, work for the food that lasts for eternal life. This is the food which the son of man will give you, because God, the Father, has put his mark of approval on him."* In John 6:35–36: *"...I am the bread of life, he who comes to me will never be hungry; he who believes in me will never be thirsty."* In Deuteronomy 8:3–4: *"He made you go hungry, and then he gave you manna to eat, food that you and your ancestors had never eaten before. He did this to teach you that man must not depend on bread alone to sustain him, but on everything that the Lord says."* In Matthew 4:4, Jesus answered to the Devil, *"The scripture says, 'man cannot live on bread alone, but needs every word that God speaks...'"*

Suppose you are praying for blessings. If God happens to tell you that though you are praying for more, what you are holding is more than enough, and He would therefore like you to bless your brother with half of what you have, how would you react? Would you praise God or would you start complaining? This question should help you understand your relationship with God. If you would complain, then your relationship or faith is built on material things, but if you would praise him, then you are a true Christian who brings honor and glory to Jesus as he sits with our Father on the throne.

The book of Kings tells us about Elijah, the servant of God, who had the power and authority to ask for fire from heaven, but the birds of the air fed him. At another incident, he was sent to a widow of Zarephath who had a handful of flour in a bowl and a drop of olive oil in a jar (1 Kings 17). This was the last meal she had. This woman never complained or refused to bless a man of God because she knew that the God in him was great and able. As a result of her trust and obedience, the bowl never ran out of flour, nor did the jar run out of oil. Both Elijah and the widow obeyed and trusted in God without complaint, and that is why they were able to receive blessings.

How many times have you rejected God's blessings because you were expecting to receive more, but you were not ready to receive what God gave to you? You start complaining to him that this is not what you asked for. How many times have you ever thought that the little that you receive is a way for the Lord to glorify Himself? But because you have heard how others have been blessed, then you want to be the same. You always go to the presence of God comparing yourself with others, and that is why you have never appreciated what God has given you. We are God's vessel, and He can glorify Himself in any way, either by blessing you with more or with little. Regardless, give glory to His name, without complaints.

Nothing impure will enter into the beautiful, shining city awaiting those who are going to wash their robes and make them white with the blood of the lamb. The blood of the lamb is not to acquire material things; it is a ticket to enter into the kingdom of God. Stop misusing the precious blood of the lamb for your own interests. Jesus did not come for you to have the best building, to drive the most expensive car in the world, and to have the best life in the world but to reconcile man with God. His coming was not fun; his life on earth until he departed was miserable. He came to suffer and to die so that at any time we may approach the throne of God with humble hearts; God will hear us and therefore bless us with His fullness. His joy should be our strength, and we should dwell in His grace forever. Let us all honor and appreciate the death and suffering of our Lord Jesus Christ.

Experience

In the early 90s, when I was still in college, someone owed me Kshs. 49.50 for certificates I had designed with my friend for a tailoring and dress-making school. He kept on promising to pay me the following Wednesday, for over one month. Then I met a Christian brother who had torn shoes. We scheduled a prayer meeting on the third day that we were to meet on the outskirts of Nairobi. That evening, I prayed bitterly for my money because I had nothing. During the night, I heard a voice assuring me that I would get the full amount the following day. But I should buy two pairs of shoes—one for me and the other one for the brother I had met. I was shown the shoes—they were black in color with a white line.

The next day, I woke up early in the morning and went to get my money. I found that the guy had put it in an envelope and was ready to leave. He gave it to me. As I was walking around, I came across a store with black shoes with a white line. I went straight into the shop to purchase them. I had made up my mind that if the money would not be enough for one pair, I would buy one pair for my brother. I was told one pair was Kshs. 25 and therefore I bought two pairs for Kshs. 48—I was given a discount.

The following day, I went to meet my friend wearing my new pair of shoes, and after prayers, I blessed him with the other pair. He was excited about the miracle I had performed for him. It is my pleasure to perform simple miracles for others because when they are happy and joyful, from their hearts, their tears of joy touch the heart of the almighty God—and in return, He blesses me with His fullness and allows me to walk in His grace and glory.

Another time, I got a casual job because I needed school fees. I worked for three weeks. God instructed me in a dream to put out wages for one week in an envelope and to bless someone who was very happy. But I was told to take away expenses that included lunch and transport every day. The second time I got a casual job, I was told to put a certain amount of money in an envelope and bless someone, and not to mention who had given the person the money. I was told to tell the person to receive the blessing.

Another time, someone owed my sister some money, and she was complaining bitterly. So in a dream God instructed me to bail that person out. I paid my sister from my pocket and told her to forgive and forget that debt because it was not worth complaining about it.

Message to Unbelievers

Imagine that tomorrow is not yours, and you will be gone. Yesterday is a dream because it is gone and tomorrow is a vision of things to come. But today is your day because you live and therefore today is the day God has made for your salvation. Do not let it go with your gift of salvation; accept Jesus today, and tomorrow you will live.

Your sins have made you a slave of your own flesh. Your body desires only for the things that are perishable, and the result is death. You have empowered your flesh and deprived your soul of the power and authority that you were given by your creator. Being a slave makes one's life miserable and desperate, filled with jealousy and hatred.

God is love and ready to forgive you. The time has come to say no to slavery and to be the master of your soul. Slavery has made you an outcast, and no one wants to be associated with you. You are overpowered by your own desire, and the driving forces make you do things that you would later regret. These driving forces never satisfy you but make you more hungry and greedy. You search for satisfaction, but you are not satisfied. You look for joy but get sorrow. You aim for happiness, but you get sadness. You look for love, but you get hate. You look for peace but get trouble. You pay for friendship but turn to enmity. You seek for self-understanding but find confusion. Being a slave does not pay because there is no freedom. You pay for all these things above but get none. Life has not been easy for you, and every time you wonder what to do next. You tend to be more violent because no one loves or cares for you. No one seems to understand you. Your heart is broken, and you seek comfort by trying many solutions. When you go to bed, you feel lonely and desperate. Being under those circumstances, your heart grieves in pain. Day and night, you go through mental torture and agony. You feel tired of living because life is no longer worth living. The Devil has lied to you that your life is over, and all that you are waiting for is judgment from God. He even confessed to you that the best way to live is to continue doing evil because you are already condemned by God, and He cannot accept you back. The sins that you have committed haunt you all the night through, confirming to you that you did them and you wonder how God could welcome you back to His Holy Place. The Devil has deceived you that you have lost the battle and cannot regain what you have lost.

The good news is that God, the creator of the universe and all the inheritance, who created you and knows the pain you go through due to slavery, loves you unconditionally. He loves you, the sinner you are. He is waiting with open hands to welcome you back. No matter what you have done or what you have gone through, today is the day of salvation. Though no one seems to care about you, and all they can do is condemn and talk about you, remember that God cares for you. He did not create you to suffer or to perish but to have eternal life. Your sins, though they may seem sticky and have left permanent spots on your heart, will be washed as white as snow by the blood of Jesus. Though your wedding gown is torn and dirty, and you may feel disqualified as a bride in the eyes of the Lord, the blood of Jesus that was shed on the Calvary will change it into something as new as it was in the beginning. The beauty and glory that you have lost will be restored as you wash yourself in the blood of Jesus. You will be loved again; you will be called the child of the highest king, the bride waiting for the bridegroom to take her home. People from different nations and races shall be blessed through you. God's blessings and anointing shall fall on you all the days of your life because you shall no longer be called an outcast or an imp, but the blessed one.

God hates your wrong doings, but loves you as a person. He hates to see you in slavery and suffering. Today, turn away from your wicked ways. Ahead of you is eternal death and suffering. Look back and answer God's call. Stretch your hand and hold His hand to be saved. The flood is coming, and you will be drawn; a strong earthquake is coming to shake the world, a strong tide will follow, and later a rain of fire will consume everything left behind, and only those who are hidden in God's heart shall be saved. Only those who are covered with the precious blood of the lamb will stand firm.

Today, God has given you another chance to repent of your sins and call upon His Holy name. Your heart is the New Jerusalem, and He is ready to rebuild the walls that have been broken. He is ready to set you free, if only you say no to your sins, no to the Devil, no to your desire, and welcome God into your life. The life is all yours. If you want to live forever and reign in His kingdom, the choice is yours today. If you want to perish, the choice is yours. God has given you free will to choose what you may think is good for you. He has blessings and curses. If you want to live, you will, but if you want death, then you will die mercilessly—the choice is yours. Today is the day of changing your life because tomorrow is not yours. Today there is an opportunity to reconcile with God, but the night is coming when nothing will be changed. When the hour of death comes, no other decision can be made.

Do not live in your past. Do not let the past steal your future. Love forgives and forgiveness ensures forgetfulness. God is love, and He is ready to forgive you and to forget. Every day marks the beginning of a new life. Death will mark the beginning of a new life, but not the end. There is a bright city where there will be no sorrow, no sadness, no mourning, no crying, no sickness, and no suffering of any kind because our God the creator of the universe lives there. There are no days or nights, no seasons or weather, no time, no weeks or months or years. The glory of the Lord God is the light of that city, and He will heal our broken hearts and wipe our tears. He is waiting patiently for you to say, "Yes Lord; I am here. Your child is listening and ready to do your will." *Do not worry about tomorrow or the next hour; worry about today or the hour you are living now.* Tomorrow's salvation will take you nowhere if you die today without washing your garments in the precious blood of Jesus. Seek the Lord when you can find Him, during the daylight, because the night is coming when death comes, and you will have no other chance to repent.

Remember, God loved us to such a degree that He gave the world the most precious gift, forgiveness of sins, by sending His son to be a sacrifice. Receive this precious gift today from God, and you will live, otherwise, you will die. Though the Devil lies to you that your time is over, you can still win God's heart. He is faithful and merciful. He sent His son to seek and find you, to set you free from slavery and to be a master of your own self and soul. There is a shining and glorious city waiting for you; just accept the invitation and do not reject it, and the peace, joy, and happiness from God shall be yours forever.

CHAPTER 20

WHY MARRIAGES BREAK

Love is a spirit like any other spirit. It has its existence in the lives we lead together. It has many dimensions. It creates magnetic forces between the hearts of two people, and it grows in an environment that is set up by friendship.

There are many things that kill love or remove the magnetic force, and then people are no longer attracted to one another. Especially for a married couple, the causes that kill their love begin as small ones. The tree of love draws water and food from both parties. Each person has his or her own interests. Each person needs to be recognized, heard, and understood.

It is the nature of human beings to fight for leadership. The consequence is that the environment becomes dry because of anger and a heaviness of the heart that makes the tree of love between the couple wither or wilt. Anger, lack of trust, betrayal, unfaithfulness, selfishness, jealousy, pride, and leadership remove the magnetic fields created by the spirit of love. All those emotions prevent the tree of love from getting its nutrients from the source, and as a result, it dies.

In most cases, couples start with disagreements on decisions to be made. The husband wants this, and the wife wants that. When they move in different directions, the Devil gets a chance to kill love and replace it with anger and hatred. When the tree of love dies, sometimes it is hard to plant another one. Once the magnetic fields are removed, then no attraction can take place. The hearts of people are surrounded by the magnetic fields created by love. The tree of love grows as one tree, but the roots join the two hearts together. Some roots come from one heart, and some from the other heart. Sometimes the tree can be uprooted from one heart and yet remain intact in the other heart. In that case, one person may have no feelings at all any longer, while the other one still has strong feelings.

The remedy for a dying love is forgiveness. Forgiveness heals the wounds that are caused and re-magnetizes the fields once again. Another way exists when the couple seeks God's guidance. Any time they want to make decision(s), they should involve God first. Whenever they differ, they should always leave the matter to God, knowing that they are ready to accept the outcome, but not be selfish. No matter whose idea wins, they should give glory and honor to God instead of criticizing one another, knowing that the success is for both of them. Swallowing pride should be the first thing to do in a marriage. No one should be proud of the outcome, but rather both should be happy, knowing that the outcome is the will of God. The couple should avoid fighting against each other; instead they should support and encourage one another, knowing that they are learning daily to become a better wife or husband. These things should be their basic goals. Thus, each person should help the other one learn how to become the best that is possible.

As God is our teacher, teaching us daily how to be better than we are, so a husband must teach his wife how to become a better wife, and the wife do the same for the husband. Each and every move must glorify God, knowing that though they are two separate beings, yet they are one in Christ. Some judgments they may receive as individuals, and others as a couple. Each person should serve the interests of the other diligently. Serving only one person's interest will result in selfishness, which gives the Devil an opportunity to steal their vision. The couple should learn how to set individual goals regarding the family, and each partner must make sure those goals are achieved.

Communication is the best weapon to use to guard well any marriage. Committing to God to bless your plans, and to do His will, will help you to fulfill God's purpose in bringing you together. Inviting God into your relationship will ensure firmness because your relationship will be built upon the strong, hard rock that cannot be shaken. Your roots will draw their nutrients from God, too.

Two people joined together can easily falter if they have no stability. But three people joined together cannot falter because is the bonds are strong. The moment two people in love begin moving in different directions, the tree will stretch and as a result, it will break up into two parts along the center. That marks the end of the relationship.

Perfect Marriage

God is a caring and loving Father, but God is not a dictator. Though God has power and authority both, He chooses to exercise authority only over us, His children. He guides us with love and care but He does not force or invade our privacy. God respects us and gives us the liberty that we deserve. He always gives us guidance, gives us enough space to breathe, accepts that we are mortal men and women, respects our decisions, and above all, respects us, His children. That is why Jesus gave the parable of the prodigal son. The prodigal son's father never gave up on his son, though the son gave up his rights. His father allowed him to choose his own way, but his father knew it was the wrong way. Yet, he never invaded nor violated his son's space. He gave his son his share as he requested because the father exercised authority, but not power. The father had a right to use his power, but then love would not have found its way. The same true with God; although He has all the power, He exercises authority over us by satisfying our heart's desires without choosing or dictating to us what to do or the best way to follow. Yet He is always ready to receive us back once we repent of our sins and choose to come back to Him. This is because He cares and loves His creations, no matter who we are or what we are or what we are doing; this does not matter to God. He loves us because we (human beings) reflect His image. Therefore, at any given time, despite the fact that we look dirty or disfigured by the things of the world, God's image is always reflected out from us. Therefore, He does not have to use power to destroy us; rather, He uses His power to strengthen and restore us to be victorious. God does not expect us to love Him but to respect and believe in Him as our caring Father. He needs appreciation from us because appreciation reflects the true love that cannot be defined with words. It does not matter how much you give, what you go through, who you are or what you have, God need only sense our appreciation and He will make everything possible for us.

Mortal fathers, men of flesh and blood, God created you for a divine purpose. You are the reflection of God and therefore God expects you to imitate or to follow in his footsteps. Fathers, use authority in your family, but not power. Love your wife and your children, too. Remember God is watching you from above, each and every move you make. Love your family with unconditional love, without expecting love back. Guide them in the right way; teach them and help them to stand on their own. Give them room to choose what they want in life, and if they make mistakes, do not despise or chase them from your presence. Always pronounce blessings on your family, no matter what your family is going through, and do not curse them. Learn how to support them; humble yourself and welcome them back in case they have chosen to go on their own way for a time. No one is a perfect father except God, but we can learn to be more like Him. Your children are your own blood, no matter what. You chose to participate in God's mission of "creating life" without being forced. Therefore, perform your duties diligently. Your family is your own life; guard them well.

Marriage is a contract entered into by the free choice of a man and a woman. Both know the consequence of their choice is to participate in the creation of life. Therefore, they must make sure they do not make the child that they create suffer in any way. It is a sin, and God does not tolerate that. God is always touched by the cries of babies or young ones, especially when they are neglected. In this regard, even if either person chooses to separate or divorce, then God expects both to bring that child up with love and care. Though a couple may choose to discontinue their relationship, the man has a responsibility to love his children and wife unconditionally. He should always respect and appreciate her, no matter what happens, knowing that it was a great favour for a woman to agree and let a man plant a seed in her womb and to let it grow for nine months.

A woman has a right to say no or to terminate it, but she chose to produce your image, your reflection. Whenever you see your child, you should always see yourself in him or her. Do not let your child suffer; that is your own image, yourself. How foolish you are to make yourself suffer by ignoring your own image, your own flesh and blood. God is watching you, men. If you father a child out of wedlock or if you are not married but create a child, that is your child, your image. Both of you may choose not to get married, but the man must respect the woman who is the mother of his child, his image and his own blood. This is not a choice but a commandment that you become bound with when you agree to participate in God's mission of creation. We are all gods, and that is why God allows us to participate in human creation. God gave us this power to create flesh and blood, the body, and for him to create the soul. After creating the body, an angel of life comes and gives life to the body in the womb. God is the only one who has the power to take the soul out of the body. The angel of death comes to take the life away from the earth. Glory is to God. Remember God sees what happen everywhere; He is watching us, whether we do good or evil.

Women, on the other hand, need to respect and be submissive to their husband. God created them in the likeness of man. She is a reflection of the man. That is why in the book of Proverbs, it says, *"Homes are made by the wisdom of woman, but are destroyed by the foolish."* The wisdom that a woman uses to make the home reflects her husband. The book of Proverbs says that it is hard to find a capable or prudent woman. Her price is worth far more than precious jewels because her husband puts his confidence in her and that ensures richness. A prudent wife is a blessing to her husband and children. She does always good to them without harming them. The qualities of a prudent wife as described in the book of Proverbs 31 are:

- *She keeps herself busy making wool and linen cloth.*

- *She brings home food from out-of-the-way places, as merchant ships do.*

- *She gets up before daylight to prepare food for her family and to tell her servant-girls what to do.*

- *She looks at land and buys it, and with money she has earned she plants a vineyard.*

- *She is a hard worker, strong and industrious.*

- *She knows the value of everything she makes, and works late into the night.*

- *She spins her own thread and weaves her own cloth.*

- *She is generous to the poor and needy. She does not worry when it snows, because her family has warm clothing.*

- *She makes bedspreads and wears clothes of fine purple linen.*

- *Her husband is well-known, one of the leading citizens.*

- *She makes clothes and belts, and sells them to merchants.*

- *She is strong and respected and not afraid of the future.*

- *She speaks with a gentle wisdom.*

- *She is always busy and looks after her family's needs.*

- *Her children show their appreciation and her husband praises her. He says, "many woman are good wives but you are the best of them all."*

That is why it is hard to place a value on a capable wife. Those qualities should be written in any woman's heart and throughout the year she should set her goals to those measures. Therefore, a man may have the authority in his home, but the woman manages the home. A man therefore must support and guide his wife, but not dictate what has to be done, because the woman has wisdom from God on how to manage the home. Why do couples fight, divorce or separate? Simply because couples do not understand their mutual roles in building a home, and therefore, conflicts of interest do arise between them.

Woman, before involving yourself in marriage, learn and understand those qualities. No man will ever tell you what he wants from you, yet he will expect you to be an excellent mother and a prudent wife. Do not lie to yourself or believe that a man needs sex to sustain him. No, men do not understand themselves and hence they do not really understand what they expect from women. When a man become frustrated or distressed in life, the first thing he does is to develop sexual desire. To a man it does not matter what type of woman he goes out with; his only concern is to satisfy his sexual desire. Men are unable to communicate. But in truth, in his heart, a man does expect and want more than sex in order to be satisfied. Surely, if wives develop those other qualities, then their husbands will be both psychologically and emotionally better.

Wives, if you want to help your husbands, then develop the above qualities. These things will bring joy, peace and glory to your husbands forever. Your value will be too high to replace, and because men are jealous, they will protect and love you in order not to lose you. In the book of Proverbs it is written, "*charm is deceptive and beauty disappears, but a woman who honours the Lord should be praised.*" Your husband will appreciate and love you because his satisfaction will not be associated with charm or beauty but with those qualities shown above. Charm and beauty are part of the initial attraction to create a desire in a man's heart, but after that they have no value. Why then do we emphasize them throughout? Simply because we do not understand the purpose of marriage and because a woman may have no vision of her ideal home. As a matter of fact, men are loving and caring husbands and fathers because they are created in the image of God.

Those women who are not married, do not give up; develop those qualities to praise God and surely someone will be attracted to you.

Husbands must be faithful to their wives. That is the only way to show appreciation, respect, and genuine love to her. The book of Proverbs 5 advises men to have the wisdom and insight that comes from God. It warns husbands against adultery because adultery destroys the home and the hard work that a wife does. This is what Proverbs tells us:

- *The lips of another man's wife may be as sweet as honey and her kisses as smooth as olive oil, but when it is all over, she leaves you nothing but bitterness and pain. Why do you want to bring pain and bitterness to your lovely wife and children?*

- *She will take you down to the world of the dead; the road she walks is the road to death. She does not stay on the road to life; but wanders off, and does not realize what is happening. Why do you husband want to bring death to your self that will cause pain and grieve to your entire family forever?*

- *Keep away from such a woman! Do not even go near her door! If you do others will gain the respect that you once had and you will die young at the hands of merciless men.*

- *Yes, strangers will take all your wealth, and what you have worked for will belong to someone else. You will lie groaning on your deathbed, your flesh and muscles being eaten away and you will say, " Why would I never learn? Why would I never let anyone correct me? I would not listen to my teachers. I paid no attention to them. And suddenly I have found myself publicly disgraced.*

- *Husband be faithful to your wife and give your love to her alone. Children that you have by other woman will do you no good. Your children should grow up to help you, not strangers.*

- *So be happy with your wife and find your joy with the girl you married-pretty and graceful as a deer. Let her charms keep you happy; let her surround you with her love. Why should you give love to another woman, my brother? Why should you prefer the charms of another man's wife?*

- *God sees everything you do. Whenever you go, he is watching you. The sins of your wickedness are a trap. You will get caught in the net of your own sins. You will die because you have no self-control. Your utter stupidity will send you to your grave.*

- *My brother, do not let shameless woman win your heart; do not go wandering after her, no matter how desperate or distressed your life is. Such a woman has been a ruin of many men and caused the death of too many to count. But if you choose to go to her house, you are on the way to the world of the dead. Actually it is a short cut to death. Are you ready to die young and leave your family lonely?*

Husbands, as God loves and cares for you, do the same for your wives. Remember you are two in one. God taught us His ways and what He expects from us. In addition to that, He sent Jesus and other prophets to teach us. As a good Father, He is always there to support us so that we can be our best, and He does this with love and care, without condemning us. He has set a standard for us to follow and He has set a good example to inspire us. Sometimes we fall short of His expectations or glory but He does not chase us from His presence; instead He corrects us with love. He does not grow weary or impatient while teaching us. That is the kind of love God wants husbands to give to their wives.

None of us is perfect in the eyes of God, but because of His love and care, He supports us every day more and more toward His perfection. It is a long process and that is why he teaches us like small children. He takes us one step at a time.

Husbands, you have responsibilities for teaching your wives to be the best wives and mothers. You need to set examples, to love them first and teach your wives and children how to love you. Asking for love first for yourself is being selfish, but giving love first and receiving it in return is what is right in the eyes of God. If one person in the family runs short of our expectations, we need to teach a better way with love and care, but not by cursing and chasing them away from our presence.

Wives, teach your husbands what you expect from them. Teach them how to become the best husbands and fathers. Remember, none of us was born with those qualities. None of us has ever been a husband or wife. Marriage is a continuous process that starts at the moment of marriage and ends when one person dies.

Don't be like unfaithful wife who commits adultery, then have bath and says to herself, "But I have done nothing wrong".

Remember that God is watching us from above.

Because women have more responsibilities than men, men are the ones who offer sacrifices to the Lord. It is not discrimination. Why do people fight in the house of the Lord or in their homes for leadership in marriage? Jesus said that if one wants to be a leader, then one must serve the others.

There is plenty to do, but the workers are few in the house of the Lord.

Remember, your joy is your own; your bitterness is your own. No one can share them with you, except God.

Love is a moving sea between the shores of two souls, a husband and a wife, Glory be to God.

CHAPTER 21

WHAT IS DEATH?

Accidents Involving School Students

I have been shocked to see the ways in which some people die. One night, I was half-asleep, and I had a vision where the agents of the Devil trapped a bus carrying students. The bus rolled several times. What surprised me was that none of those students were seriously hurt to the extent of dying, but as soon as the bus stopped rolling, I saw the Devil's agents running from a nearby bush towards the bus. At first, I thought they were angels going to rescue those students because they were dressed in white. But they were holding the students upright and then injecting them in the head with a certain chemical that I could not recognize. These students then fell into a coma before they died.

Actually, this is what happens in most accidents, everywhere.

Visiting the Mortuary

One of my sisters, who is a nurse, moved to Nairobi and got a house in the city mortuary compound. One weekend, she had to travel home, and she had to leave her baby and the maid, who was very new. Therefore, she requested me to go and spend the weekend at her house in her absence, and I agreed. I went through the main gate to her house compound with a lot of fear. During the night, I did not even want to look through the windows because I thought the dead people would be walking around the house. During the night, the Holy Spirit of God took control of me, and I was taken outside the house. I found someone outside whom I could not recognize, and he told me to follow him.

There were two blocks for preserving the dead bodies. The door opened, and we went into the first block from the main gate. I saw the dead bodies; some had overstayed and others were very fresh. What shocked me was that the fresh bodies still contained some of the victims' souls. Out of curiosity, I asked the gentleman with me why they were not dead and what they were doing in the mortuary. He looked at me, smiled, and then he said, "Charles, to be dead means that the soul has completely left the body and has no connection, or the soul is still in the body but unconscious. During the accident, the soul is fully conscious, preoccupied with many things, without expecting to meet death. Therefore, due to the severity of the accident, the body may completely fail to function, and you people declare someone dead while the soul remains fully conscious within the body. Those souls were looking for mercy, and they can talk. After some days, they will give up and became unconscious because they can no longer gain strength.

"When some people die, their souls remain unconscious within their bodies; others get out of their body and begin roaming around while the holy ones go to paradise, led by angels. When the holy ones die, their death opens a gate to a bright world where the angels are waiting to take them home (paradise). But those who remain in the grave are surrounded by darkness; they are not warm or cold. Their case is to be determined during the Day of Judgment. Those who go on roaming the world are the rebellious ones. Their souls are fully dedicated to the Devil.

What Causes Death?

God gave power to man to create flesh but not life. When a man and woman come together as husband and wife, they do not actually create life so much as they shelter it. God sends his angels of life to give life to the flesh created, and thereafter the infant's body begins to function. Life is not the heart. There is an angel of life and an angel of death. Therefore, the soul gives light and lives in the body and also prevents the body from decaying. Once the soul is unconscious or leaves the body, then the body has no life, and therefore it starts decaying.

Death is not something forced, but most of those who die are willing to do so or have been longing for it due to various circumstances. Before death comes, the victims are put into certain circumstances, such that the only solution they might have is death.

I have seen people in spirit being bitten by dangerous snakes and other inexplicable creatures that cause either sudden death or a death that arrives shortly after. Floods draw some people, while others fall into a deep pit. People are not aware of these creatures, but they can make people desperate and hopeless.

What shocked me most were the AIDS and HIV cases. I saw young people in a field in the city of the cities. They were told to line up. I saw the mist that covered their souls leaving them with rust or burns and bruises—fresh wounds on their souls. This mist had no formula but could cover anyone. Only a few people were not affected. As I was watching, I asked myself why it had to happen. Then I heard a voice saying to me, "Charles, do not be surprised. Not all who are affected are sinners, and that is why they are suffering. Most of them are innocent, but the prophecy must be fulfilled. These are the last days that the prophets talked about. The world has turned away from God.

The Devil has lied to many that there is no God. The world today is full of evil. This is exactly what happened when the Israelites turned away from God in the wilderness. God sent snakes to kill people by biting them. Those snakes did not choose but could bite anyone they came across, except Moses and those who were faithful to God. Without this deadly disease, the world could be worse seven times over than Sodom and Gomorrah. But because God is merciful with what He has created, he has shortened the days of many so that they could inherit the kingdom of God. But those who are faithful will be clean. The suffering itself leads others to turn to God for help and to repent their sins because God said that none of His people would perish." Therefore, this disease is not a punishment for the sinners but a way to control and draw people back to God. We are put in chains of slavery by our wickedness. If people remain faithful to God, surely God would not allow such calamities to fall on mankind.

How I Carried Someone's Baby for One Week

A certain lady, whom I knew very well, was married and pregnant. A few weeks before her delivery, she went to the hospital and was advised that she would need surgery because there was no way she could have delivered in the normal way. She called and asked me to meet her in town. When I met her, she looked worried. After general talks, she told me that she was worried because she had to go through surgery, but she said that she was not ready to lie on the surgical table. She wanted to deliver normally. I told her not to worry but to allow God to glorify Himself according to His will.

When I went home, I included her request in my evening prayers. Then during the night, something amazing happened. I was half-asleep, and the same lady appeared. I could see the baby. The baby was tied up with dirty rags, and demons were waiting for the baby at the time of delivery to kill it. The only way to save the baby was to be operated on spiritually. Then I underwent an operation, and the baby was fitted on my right side so that her womb could be cleaned. I was instructed to remain with the baby for seven days and not to leave the house. When I woke up, I felt very uncomfortable and tired.

On the seventh day, in my dream, I felt very relieved and refreshed during the night. The next day, I got a message that the lady had delivered a health baby boy, normally. No operation was done.

CHAPTER 22

WHAT IS A SOUL?

A soul is the power or energy that God has put into a human body to give it life. It is in the form of spirit, which we cannot see. It does not reside in one part of the body but keeps on moving throughout the blood. It can leave the body, go to another place or world, and come back into it as long as it remains connected. It happens so fast because it can move at the speed of light. That is why sometimes, one can go to heaven and spend three days but come back to the flesh and only minutes may have passed. Most of us have experienced that in a dream. In some dreams, we spend days or we do many activities, but when we wake up, we find we have slept for only thirty minutes. Sometimes a soul can travel into the future and understand how the future will be; that is a vision.

The soul has no language barriers. There is only one language understood by all souls, or perhaps the soul has the ability to understand all languages. The soul has unlimited power and the ability to perform anything. God granted this power and authority during the time of creation. On the other hand, a soul on earth operates in human flesh, which is ruled by a human mind. Human minds are limited in terms of power, their ability to perform, language, and mobility, among other things. Our souls desire for the things that are spiritual, but our minds desire material or physical things. The soul has the ability to see beyond what the naked eye cannot see and has the ability to gather information from different places in an instant. The soul then interprets and communicates to the mind at a very high speed. Most of the time, much of the information is lost due to overflow. Our minds are always busy. That is why sometimes we dream but we cannot remember what the dream was about. At the spirit level, we understand that we had a dream, but at the human level, we cannot recall it, for our minds are always preoccupied.

The soul and mind must communicate in harmony. The soul should be the master of the mind but not vice versa. Between the human level and the spiritual level, there is a gap. This gap cannot remain as a vacuum. It is in this gap that either the spirit of God resides or the spirit of the Devil. The mind receives information from the soul and also either from the spirit of God or from an evil spirit.

The spirit of God empowers the soul to act at its fullness because they are identical. But the evil spirit empowers the mind or the flesh.

Any idea that is communicated to the mind has power in it. Since the mind has the ability to process and store it, the idea can be destructive or creative, depending on its source. This means that the more it processes an idea, the more the idea generates the power to force or pressure the mind (flesh) to act. It is a driving force.

There are seven evil spirits, and the demons are in spirit form, too. Ideas generated by those evil spirits, or demons, suppress the soul and empower the flesh to do what is wrong or evil. There is only one good spirit of God. God communicates through his Holy Spirit or the angels. Any idea generated by Holy Spirit, soul, or angels overpowers the flesh and forces the flesh to do what is good. The Holy Spirit or soul communicates in an orderly and peaceful manner. It creates a divine peace that goes beyond human understanding. A person with the Holy Spirit will desire to do good or right in the eyes of God and always thinks about God. But those who have allowed other spirits to lead them will find themselves doing what is wrong in the eyes of God. Jesus said that the greatest commandment is to love God with all the mind and soul.

Some people have been dominated by several spirits or demons and therefore receive much information or hear many voices at the same time. In the process, their mind becomes confused in terms of how to interpret that information, or store it. As a result, they become mentally ill. Luke 8:28–31: "*When the man possessed with demons saw Jesus, he gave a loud cry, threw himself down at his feet, and shouted, 'Jesus, son of the Most High God! What do you want with me? I beg you, do not punish me!' He said this because Jesus ordered the evil spirit to go out of him. Many times it had seized him, and even though he was kept a prisoner, his hands and feet fastened with chains, he would break the chains and be driven by the demon out into the desert. Jesus asked him, 'What is your name?' He answered, 'My name is mob' because many demons had attacked him.*"

In Luke 11:24–26, Jesus explained how one becomes possessed with seven evil spirits, "*When an evil spirit goes out of a person, it travels over dry country looking for a place to rest. If it cannot find one, it says to itself, I will go back to my house. So it goes back and finds the house clean and tidy. Then it goes out and brings seven other spirits even worse than itself, and they come in and live there. So when it is all over, that person is in a worse state than he was at the beginning.*"

God gave us free will to choose the voice that we want to hear. That is why we are held accountable for anything that we do. The Devil will not be accused for our own sins, but we will pay the price or face the judgment alone unless we repent.

When the preachers are preaching, some minister to the soul and others to the mind. Ministering to the soul results in the repentance of sins and the true worship of the Most High God. That is the divine or anointed preaching from God. Other preachers entertain the flesh (mind) by telling people what they want to hear. Those are preachers that are either planted by the Devil or have personal interests.

The other issue that empowers mind addresses the type of food we eat. Fasting keeps our body healthy and draws us close to God because it empowers the soul, as well.

CHAPTER 23

WHO IS RIGHT...CHRISTIANS OR MUSLIMS?

One day I became eager to know why we have Christians and Muslims, yet they have slight differences. They believe in the same God, and their faith is based on the Old Testament. Both believe in the Day of Judgment and the coming of Jesus Christ for the second time. Actually, what amazed me was that the Koran talked more about Mary, the mother of Jesus, in regards to the birth of Christ than the Bible itself.

After three days, I heard someone telling me to wake up and follow him in a dream. To wake up means to go out of my body. We went into a wilderness, and then he told me, "Charles, wait and see what is going to happen." Then, after a little while, I saw two groups appear, one on the left and the other one on the right side.

He introduced the two groups as Christian worshippers on one side and Muslim worshippers on the other side. The two groups started praying, and the prayers from both groups were accepted. Then I asked both groups to ask for fire from heaven, and the group that received fire would be the group that worshipped the true God. Both groups asked for fire, and both groups received fire. I became more confused than before.

I asked the gentleman who was with me to explain to me the difference. He looked at me, smiled, and then said, "Charles, the way you are testing those two groups is wrong. Both groups believe in the living God, the Most High King, the God of the universe. At that high level, both groups have no difference. Suppose you bring the Devil here. He will also receive anything he asks for because he believes there is a God who is the source of his power and strength."

"Then what is the difference?" I asked. He said, "Jesus has been given the power and authority to rule the world. He was crowned to be the king in the house of the Most High God. All the knees shall bow to him. He has the power and authority from above to judge the world. The Devil, demons, and evil spirits are cast or rebuked in the name of Jesus Christ. Those who are called by his name are given the power and authority to rule and judge the world. Just as the Israelites were the chosen few during the time of Moses, Christians are the chosen few in his kingdom. The prophets and holies will be kings, but Jesus will be the overall king. Through Jesus, the power of darkness was defeated." Then he left without answering my question. That is why I respect all religions, so long as they preach about righteousness and goodness.

We are all different but one in God.

CHAPTER 24

GOD'S BLESSINGS CAN TURN INTO A CURSE

In the late 1980s, one of my sisters was not getting along well with her husband. At that time, they had separated. In the 1990s, God sent me a message that if she waited upon Him, her family would be together once again. All that she needed to do was to believe and trust in God, and everything would be well. I visited her and delivered this message to her, though she did not believe it. Furthermore, she had known me since the day I was born, and she could not understand what I was telling her or imagine favor from God. I could see that her heart was full of doubt, but I tried to share some verses in the Bible to build her trust.

It took a little while, but then she lost hope. She never listened to me and instead did what she thought was good for her. I tried to dedicate my prayers to her for God to change her ways, but God's response was, "My love for your sister is unconditional but for her to receive my blessings, she needs to come back to me. She needs to stand in my promises and wait for me patiently. I can bless her to fulfill my promise, but if she is not on my side, then she will not enjoy those blessings." I tried to talk to her because I knew the consequences, but instead she rejected my instructions.

In the early 90s, I was half-asleep when I saw heaven open. I saw the throne of God and a big snake that was green in color; it was coiled in every branch of a huge tree. I heard a voice asking from the throne, "What can we do to make Charles's sister go back to her home?" Then I heard God commanding in heaven, "I want to send you to Charles's sister's husband and bite him. The time has come for me to fulfill the promise by reuniting Charles's sister's family." I looked behind me to see who was being told this, but I only saw a huge green snake coiled in a very huge tree. I could not see the tail or the head of the snake.

At once, the snake jumped as if it was just lying on the ground. I could see it flying across the sky, and I was left speechless. He said to me, "Charles, this is the weapon I use for those who refuse to do my will." What amazed me was the way the snake uncoiled within a second and jumped. It was a thousand feet long after it uncoiled. When I woke up I tried to pray to stop it, but it was too late. A few years later, her husband fell ill.

During the time her husband was ill, my sister went to see him. After observing his condition, she called me early in the morning before I woke up. But before she made a call, God had informed me about her call in a dream. In my dream, I saw her coming running towards me and before she arrived, I heard the voice from above telling me, "Charles, I am angry with your sister. I am the author of life and death and no one is supposed to ask whether one is to die or to live in order to take advantage of me. That is using my name in vain. I am the one who chose and uplifted you for my work, not for the work of your family. She refused to believe you when I sent you to her. This is what is going to happen." A curtain was removed, and I saw her husband lying in a hospital bed dead, their first-born son in another bed in the same room, dying, and then my sister in the same room but healthier, though in the process of dying. I cried with a loud voice in the dream, "Lord, have mercy on her." Then God prolonged her life but refused to prolong the lives of her husband and son because they were already dead in the dream.

Before I completed my dream, I heard a knock at my bedroom door and a voice told me that I had a phone call. I went to answer the phone, and it was my sister. She asked me to pray to God to find out whether her husband was going to die because he was very sick. This was one of the most painful moments I have ever gone through. I could not answer her; instead, I told her that to give life or to take it away is God's responsibility, and therefore we have no right to ask about it. We can only pray for God's will to prevail.

Then I replaced the receiver. My heart was filled with grief and agony knowing what was waiting for her, but God is just. God called me to follow His ways, not for Him to follow my ways. He did not call me to contradict him. Therefore, I could not go back to God because the case was already concluded. Though later I mourned for my sister's family with fasting, it was too late. I gave it up and waited for God's will to be done.

It did not take more than two weeks before her husband passed away. Later, after a couple of years, she fell sick, and everybody gave up on her. I knew the promise that God had made to me that she would fall sick but God would prolong her life. I thank God for that because He is faithful. She is healthy and working at the time that I write this book. Glory be to God.

When her husband died, his soul was very stubborn. Every day, he could come and call out for his wife and first-born son. I had to detain his soul somewhere and fence it so that he could not come back to claim his family until the Day of Judgment.

Unfortunately, their first-born son fell sick and was admitted to the same hospital but later passed away, in late 2004. The prophecy had come to pass.

This incident taught me a lot. Some of the things that I learned were that God's word must come to pass, no matter what. Also, my faithfulness or trust in God cannot save others during their times of trouble. It can only save me. Also, God is just and requires us to be just, too. He did not call us to contradict Him but to be His instrument, to follow Him but not to lead Him.

CHAPTER 25

KENYAN ROAD OF DEMOCRACY

A lot of things in Kenya have happened, but the most interesting of them all is her road to democracy. Kenya is a small country, but her people fear God most. The majority of Kenyans are committed Christians and Muslims. It is one of the few blessed nations in the world where the Christians, Muslims, and other religions speak without fighting. It is one of the few countries where Christians and Muslims sit together to deliberate issues like brothers and sisters. They eat at the same table and drink as brothers and sisters. They share both bad and good moments. They believe there is more to share beyond religion and cultural differences, and more to learn from each other. They all need each other because they are brothers and sisters, and they belong to the same community.

Kenya has really suffered during the last few decades. People were demonstrating all over the country now and then. Violence erupted among the tribes, including murder, looting, devil worship, and corruption among government officials.

At that time, I was constantly praying for my country Kenya, praying for God's intervention because of the suffering of the innocent people. In the early 1990s, before the '92 elections, I saw in my dream former President Moi at his home. He was eating traditional African food, and he was without security. He was very happy and relaxed. There was a person with me whom I could not recognize, but I asked him why the former President Moi had no security and seemed relaxed. He said, "Kenya is my country, through which I have chosen to bless many nations. But the Kenyans are ignorant and do not understand the purpose that I have for them. Through this oppression, they will seek me with sincere hearts. They will cry, and I will hear their cry and heal their nation. When that time comes, your president Moi will step down peacefully and a new leader will take over. It will be just like a dream, and the whole system will be restored. Kenyans will not believe it because it will happen so fast, but they will know that I heard their cry and came to rescue them. They will call me, and I will answer them because they will be my people."

Then I asked him whether the former President Moi by then deserved the kingdom of God or not. He said, "Salvation is a seed planted in human hearts. No matter what they do due to the influence of circumstances, this power reminds them to repent when they are alone. Charles, to answer your question, go and ask him what salvation is."

I went straight to where former President Moi was seated, pulled out a chair, and sat down next to him. Then I asked him to explain what he understood about salvation. The former President Moi looked at me, stopped eating, and then looked down. He said, "Charles, I feel bad that leadership made me do things that do not please God. I love God and desired always to serve God with a clean heart." At that time, he said, he could not control himself, and then he started crying bitterly. I just looked at him helplessly. I patted his shoulders and said to him, "Do not worry, because Jesus loves you." We prayed, and I left believing that he was a child of God. Since then, I have prayed for him every day and night, and I no longer criticize him.

I have learned how to respect political leaders as children of God despite the circumstances in which they might find themselves. I love them all and pray for them, but they need to change because they are God's vessel and are meant to lead God's people diligently.

Before the election in 1992, I was half-asleep when I heard someone wake me up in spirit to anoint the leader in my dream. I woke up in a dream and followed someone that I could not recognize. Then we went out to a field where I met all the presidential candidates. We sat at a table and started calling one candidate at a time, with the exception of former President Moi because he was already in power. What surprised me was that I could see hatred, bitterness, greed, anger, and pride. Mr. Kibaki, whom I found fit, was the third person to be interviewed. He was humble and clean-hearted but undecided. He lacked confidence at that time. The burden was too heavy and could have crushed him.

After the interview, the person seated next to me asked me who was worthy to take over the leadership, but I replied, "None of them." So former President Moi was given two more years. Two years meant two terms and each term is five years.

The next day, when I woke up, I could not believe that there would be no change for the next ten years. I prayed sincerely, rejecting the decision that I had made in the dream.

Another night, I was asleep when President Kibaki appeared in my dream. He was at the top of the hill, and I was at the bottom. I heard someone telling me, "Charles, you have another chance. Go up the hill and greet Mr. Kibaki by hand. Tell him that he has gained favor in the eyes of the Lord to rule over my people. If you are able to pass the message to him in spirit, then your decision will be reversed."

I tried to climb the hill, but it was very slippery. I tried several times until I gave up. I heard the voice telling me, "Charles, do not worry or feel guilty. The decision you made was the right one because Kenya is not ready for change. Any change now may result in bloodshed. I promised to complete a peaceful transition when the right time comes."

When I woke up, I was not content but continued asking, *what if.* During that time, in my dreams, I was given a third chance. I was instructed to go physically to deliver the message to him in person. I wrote it nicely, and the next day I went to a continental house where he had an office. I asked how I could see him. I was told that the only way was to go and camp in his office. I went there for three consecutive days, and then I gave it up and allowed the will of God to take place.

I revealed to my sister Lucy the person who would take over the government. During the elections, she voted for him and because the outcome was negative, she was angry with me. She asked me why I had lied to her. I told her that I had not been talking about the elections, but I said that when Moi stepped down, the person that would succeed him would be Kibaki. General elections do not mean it is God's right time. God's right time is coming.

During the elections, I did not go to vote because I knew the outcome already. When the results were announced, they were exactly the same, with President Moi resuming the office once again.

In the second election, it was the same; President Moi resumed the office for the second term. But the third time, in 2002, President Moi stepped down and President Kibaki took over the government. The transition was so peaceful—such that not only Kenyans were amazed, but also the whole world. I understand that former President Moi is a born-again Christian. Glory is to God because he does not judge us by our actions but by our hearts. Actions reflect circumstances, but the heart reflects who we are, in truth. He is a just God.

CHAPTER 26

POPE JOHN PAUL'S REVELATION

When Pope John Paul II came to Kenya, Nairobi in September 1995, God gave me a message to take to him. The message was very simple. "Charles, tell the Pope to cleanse himself because I am coming for him soon. He will know my coming because he will fall from the seat at the pulpit more than twice and lose strength. The third time I will come for him." After I woke up I said, "God, it is impossible. I will not be allowed to go near him." In fact, instead of going to Uhuru Park where he was conducting mass, I went to visit my friends to avoid passing the message to him. But I was touched after I read his will and found that he was longing to go home. I regretted not making an effort to see him to pass on this message.

I had a lot of confusion in my head about my life and mission until the death of Pope John Paul. I knew I had no time left after learning of his death. A week after Pope John was promoted from human glory to spiritual glory, I had two dreams that disturbed me most regarding him.

On Monday the 7th, after the Pope's death, I was traveling by bus from Boston to New York. At around 1 p.m., I fell asleep on the bus because the journey was long. In my dream, Pope John Paul II appeared to me with my personal message. He called me by name, delivered the message, and disappeared. The message said, "Charles, God has anointed you. Do what God sent you to do." I woke up immediately from the dream very frightened. It was around 1:30 p.m., and I did not sleep again after that.

The next day, on Tuesday the 8th, I was at home. At around 2 p.m., I felt sleepy and lay on my bed. I was half-asleep when I saw the remains of the Pope in a coffin that was laid on a table in a small closed room. Then the people who had brought him inside left to join the multitude of people outside, but they locked the room from the outside. I asked them why they were locking the room from the outside while I was still inside, but none of them answered me. Now I could hear people talking from the outside but none could hear me calling them to open the doors. Then suddenly the small room was filled with a glorious bright light, and someone (a gentleman) appeared. He stood on one side of the table, and I was standing on the other side. He was dressed like a priest in a robe with a white scarf hanging around his shoulders. The scarf fell on the floor, and I picked it up and hung it around his shoulders again without saying a word. Then I went back to my position and looked at the remains of the Pope. I called to him, "Pope, why are you still sleeping (dead)? Wake up." He woke up and sat up, spiritually, but he was still very weak and weary. After a short moment, he stepped down, though I could still see his remains (flesh) in the casket. What amazed me was the glory the Pope had. He looked young, handsome, and his face was glittering with a lot of joy.

At that time, I saw two doors open, one on my left side and the other on my right side. Then I saw the gentleman directing the Pope out of one of these doors. Neither the gentleman nor the pope said a word. I left the room through the door on my side, but I could still see the remains of the Pope on the table.

It is true that when we die, an angel of God comes for us in a bright light to take those who are righteous to paradise. Though his remains were still on the table, the Pope (the soul) went with His maker. Glory be to God

PART III

CHAPTER 27

WHO IS THE DEVIL?

In God's kingdom, the Devil was given the power and the authority over all angels in heaven. He was an archangel, the commander and angel of fire. This did not satisfy him; rather he wanted to be worshipped and adored. The Devil became furious and refused to obey God after the creation of Adam and Eve. God created Adam in His likeness and gave him dominion over everything that He created in this world. God gave Adam the ability to think and the liberty to explore so that he could develop the universe so as to continue with creation. Then God commanded all the angels to serve man and worship him, as he was like God. The Devil rejected this command and instead chose to reject God's leadership. The Devil also convinced a group of angels to worship him instead, and he oppressed the angels who refused. He could not understand why God created man after everything else, yet made man equal to God.

The Devil thought that he was second from God, and no one else should be worshipped above him except God. He crowned himself because he became jealous. Therefore, two groups of angels opposing each other were formed in heaven, the good and the evil ones. The good ones were under the angels Michael and Gabriel, while the Devil was the leader of the evil group. Michael humbled himself before God and requested that the Devil be removed from power because he was oppressing them. God gave Michael the authority and power to remove the Devil from authority, and he (Michael) became a new leader or commander of the angels in heaven.

The angels were created to serve God and then their roles were extended to serve human beings. That is why we are special because we are greater than angels, though man was created last. God is the king of the universe and man is the king of the world, but the angels are servants or messengers.

When God created the universe, God put man in charge of the world and gave him power and authority over all that he created on it. He built a little heaven on earth for him—the Garden of Eden—and made him the king to rule the world. God did not have to create another spiritual being because the angels were already there. He thought it was wise to create beings with flesh so that in case they rebelled, their lives could be terminated easily. The Devil was not pleased by God's plan, as he was hungry for power and authority. He was looking for somewhere to stay, since he was no longer entertained in heaven. With his evil thoughts, he decided to deceive man in order to separate him from God.

The Devil knew that the consequences of sin were slavery and death for mankind. This was a golden opportunity for him to take control of the world and its inheritance, including mankind.

The immediate consequences of sin are the deprivation of the power and authority one possesses, with a long suffering, both physically and spiritually. As a result, one tends to lose everything. This was how man surrendered his kingdom, and the rights that God had granted him, to the Devil. That was the basic reason why the Devil deceived man— to destroy the relationship between God and man, to bring death to mankind, and to take away all that belonged to man.

This is why even today the Devil deceives mankind to sin, so that he can remain in power and have authority and power throughout the ages. When the prophets and servants of God, including Jesus, came to this world, they retained power and authority because they refused to be misled by the Devil. They become masters of their lives instead of slaves to their own sins. They lived a righteous life, and they had godliness in them. God restored His kingdom in them, and therefore they were standing in the promises of the Lord. They were able to exercise authority from above by performing miracles. Jesus said that the kingdom of God is at hand, and He has been given power and authority from above.

When Moses was called by God and accepted to live a godly life, he repossessed the power and authority that he had lost. God made him to be like Him, and his brother Aaron became his prophet. He performed miracles and other wonders. When Jesus was taken to the wilderness, the Devil was waiting to tempt him. One of the temptations given to Jesus was to kneel and worship the Devil himself and he (the Devil) would give the earthly kingdom to Jesus. Jesus said no, because he knew that it was his right to inherit the Earthly kingdom at the time of his birth; it was not to be given by the Devil, who had stolen it from mankind. Jesus said that He came to find and seek that which was stolen by the Devil. He further said that if we believe and live according to the standards set by God, then we shall receive more power and authority to do greater things. What limits us from receiving the power and authority from God is our own iniquities. No one is an exception. Everyone could be restored their power and authority, if only we surrender ourselves to the will of God.

God created the earthly kingdom and blessed man with it. God does not take His blessings back if one decides to walk away from Him.

Now, since God's plan was for the earthly kingdom to last forever, He had to send a savior who could save the world from man's enemy. That is why Jesus was to be born like any other human being, to suffer and to die in order to take back the kingdom. He suffered our iniquities. He was crowned to be the king, and this is why he said that the kingdom of the world and heaven was given to him. He is coming to judge the world and to eliminate anything that is evil or taboo. Through one man (Adam) the world was condemned and lost God's glory, and through one man (Jesus) the world was saved and gained God's glory.

The Devil came to steal and destroy the relationship between man and God. The Devil is not interested in you as a person; he is interested in depriving you of your peace and replacing it with suffering. The most precious gift that makes man remain in his senses is peace. The Devil tries to destroy your peace through death, sickness, violence, discouragement, mourning, sadness, and shocking news. As a man, you need to put on your armor and sustain your sense of peace to remain in your senses. Peace brings happiness and joy, which draws you closer to the presence of God. When one approaches the throne of God with a humble and sincere heart asking forgiveness, God is ready to forgive. The forgiveness restores the relationship that was lost by sins. It also restores the kingdom, power, and authority that God gave freely to mankind. God is Love, and Love forgives, no matter how sinful we are.

It is time for us to stand up and humble ourselves before the almighty God to remove the Devil from power. We have the right to take back what the Devil has stolen from us. The whole world is suffering because we gave up our rights to our enemy, a destroyer, and a killer, the Devil. Why do we allow ourselves to suffer? Why cannot we tell the Devil that it is enough? The world was created for us, and therefore we have the right to chase the Devil away from this world. What are we waiting for? All that we need is to say no to the slavery of our own sins and focus on the power and authority that God has granted to us freely. We need to cleanse and humble ourselves before the almighty to recapture what we lost.

It does not matter what background we come from because God loves us all, the sinners that we are. We are all the children of the living Most High God. We need to acknowledge Him as the creator of the universe, and worship and glorify Him. We have one thing in common despite our background—we are all fighting one spiritual enemy, the Devil and his followers— as human beings. We go through the same suffering every day. God is ready to forgive us.

We are all different but we are the same in the eyes of God. The diversity among us beautifies the world and makes it interesting to live in. But the Devil uses that diversity to convince some people that they are more superior or less than others, in order to create enmity among us. We are beautiful creatures in the face of the world. God is the tree, and we are all branches. Therefore, we should appreciate one another, knowing that one of us is a part of God. We should not discriminate against others for any reason. We are what we are because God created each one of us for a unique purpose. It does not matter whether we are black or white, poor or rich, genius or idiot, fluent in other languages, religious among others—we make the world to be the way it is. Why do we agree to serve the Devil by carrying out his evil mission of destroying man and the world? Why do we kill our brothers and sisters? Why do we bear false witness and steal from our brothers and sisters? Others make you what you are. God is for us all.

God has made it possible for a man to recover all that he has lost and to reconcile with Him through forgiveness of sin. For so God loved the world that He gave his beloved son so that whoever believed in Him would not perish but would have eternal life, as it is written in the Bible. Jesus is the truth, and the way to recover that which we have lost is to restore the relationship between God and us. Glory be to God on High.

CHAPTER 28

Who is Jesus?

Jesus was the first to be created by God before any other creation in the universe. His purpose was to offer sacrifice to God. Later, God created the Devil, and all other heavenly bodies. He gave power and authority to Lucifer, the Devil, to rule the angels in heaven. Later, he rebelled from God at the creation of the world, though he was still in heaven by then.

When God created the universe and its inheritance, he made man in his own likeness and put him in charge of the world with a physical form. He placed both the tree of life and knowledge in the garden and forbid Adam to eat of their fruits. God wanted to test whether man would be faithful and obedient to Him. Then God commanded all the angels to adore mankind. This did not impress Lucifer, as he had power and authority over the angels. Being in heaven for long and close to God, Lucifer could understand the weakness of mankind. Lucifer knew how to weaken the relationship between God and man in order to inhabit the world. Lucifer knew what God liked and hated.

The main purpose of the Devil is to make man annoy God, so that God would withdraw His presence from man. In this way, the Devil could have a golden opportunity to possess the world and put man into captivity.

Lucifer asked permission to lead man astray, and this was granted. When God came and found that Adam had done what God had forbidden, He was not happy. Despite the fact that man had broken God's law, man went ahead and blamed God by pinpointing the woman that he had been given. Also, man was trying to run away or hide from the presence of God instead of repenting. In other words, man had already judged himself before he had been judged by God. That is why God asked the man who told him that he was naked. The man was not sorry for what he had done, and this made God furious because the man had trusted Lucifer. This means that the man had no trust in God at all. Out of anger, God cursed man and the ground that brings life forth into the world. Everything that God created in this world became subject to God's curses. God took away the Garden of Eden from the face of the world, together with the privileges man used to enjoy, and instead replaced them with everlasting suffering and agony.

Thereafter, the man (Adam) started his hardship in this world. He had to work hard in order to get something to eat. He became self-sufficient and forgot about the purpose that God had for him. He left the entire door open, and it was at that time that the enemy, or the Devil with his followers (demons), possessed or dominated the whole world. Man lost all that he had and instead became a slave to sin. He no longer walked on the road of righteousness but instead went astray, where he became confused, desperate, and was put into captivity by the enemy. After some time, man began multiplying, and the more he increased, the more he began to go astray.

Jesus, being in the grace of God, asked God to spare the life of mankind. He sympathized with the misery man experienced and the suffering he was going through. He pleaded with God and promised that he could restore the relationship between man and God. The only way to end human suffering was to sacrifice himself to the world. God could not just grant the kingdom to Jesus, and therefore he had to pay the price by partaking of our suffering and death.

God loved the world, as it is written in Genesis that after creation God loved His creation. He agreed to send His son Jesus to suffer and to die for our sins. God promised the world a wonderful councilor, a messiah, Emmanuel (meaning God with us), a lamb that would take away the sins of the world, a good shepherd, and a true servant. Jesus is the Son of God, as he was the first to be created and the only one in the grace of God, though all the angels and mankind are also sons of God. God is a Father or creator to all that He has created. God has no physical form but is in spirit.

In order to carry out his mission, Jesus had to have a physical form. When he came to the world, he was not a king. When Jesus was born, the enemies were aware of him and wanted to eliminate him. That is why the three wise men from the east were led by a star. The star disappeared when they reached Herod's palace. Jesus was born in a manger because he was a holy child. The manger was holy since no man had ever slept or sat on it. In the big hotels and guesthouses, that is where sins were jumping like frogs. God could not allow Jesus to be contaminated with sins at birth. Jesus came as a shepherd, and that is why the shepherds were given the message before about their counterparts.

Jesus walked on the road of righteousness. He felt pain, suffered, and enjoyed life like any normal human being. He understood us (mankind) and taught us about the grace and love of God. As he gained favor from God, he gained hatred from people. He taught about the simple way to gain God's favor because God Himself is simple. The religious leaders at that time misinterpreted his messages and never listened to him. They decided to eliminate him so that people would not be confused about God. This was because he was gaining more popularity and could perform miracles in order to glorify the name of the living God. They tried to eliminate him in the name of preserving the interest of their god.

The last day came for Jesus, and he had to bear the pain and humiliation for the sake of us. At that time, God had forgotten Jesus. He did not want to see the pain Jesus was going through because He did not want to pour His anger upon those who were prosecuting and crucifying His son. The reason for his 18-hour suffering was a test to see whether Jesus could have cursed mankind. When he prayed, "Father, forgive them, for they know not what they do," he passed his test. His Father was proud of him.

After the resurrection of Jesus, he ascended into heaven where all the angels waited for him; all the saints who lived in heaven came to meet their king. Through his tolerance, we were saved from the wrath of God.

He was hosted in a king's style. God the Father dressed him in a crown, and he was given a shepherd's rod to rule God's people because he was made a king in the house of God. He was given power and authority to judge the world.

The Christians of today break the greatest commandments of God because Jesus did not come to replace his Father but to teach the world about God. There is only one God, and he tolerates no rivals. God never promised the world another god but a messiah, a savior, a lamb who takes away the sins of the world. A sacrifice is not greater than the one who offers the sacrifice.

Jesus taught the world about his Father, who is also our Father. He taught us how to address or approach Him while praying. He promised us that if we remain faithful, we should receive more power than he had. He also commanded us to love God with all our minds and deeds. Jesus almost gave up. He also cried out at the cross, "Why have you forsaken me?" But when he remembered that he had accomplished his mission, he was filled with joy.

Those who think that God came into the world to suffer and die are wrong. God could not degrade Himself and die. If this were true, then it would mean there was a time when there was no God in the universe. God said, heaven is my dwelling place and the earth is my footstep. He is God who changes not—yesterday, and today, and tomorrow remain the same. Jesus is the shining morning star that sheds its light on human hearts. He is the lion of Judah.

We as human beings need to understand how to forgive one another. We cannot pray to God to forgive others and yet fail to forgive them. If we pray to God, we should be ready to carry the burden, no matter what comes our way, in order to set them free. We should forgive first, and then ask God to forgive our wrongdoers later.

CHAPTER 29

WHO IS GOD?

There is only one God, the creator of the Universe and all its inheritance. Those who have more than one god are wrong. The Lord God created man in his own likeness with the exception that man could not differentiate right from wrong. It is evident that the heavenly bodies are like God. God did the work of creation, though he informed the heavenly bodies of his intentions. In Genesis 1:26-27: *"And now we will make human beings; they will be like us and resemble us. They will have power over all dominions."* So God created human beings, making them to be like him. He created a male and later, a female. In Genesis 3:22–24: *"The Lord God said, now the man has become like one of us and has knowledge of what is good and what is bad. He must not be allowed to eat fruit from the tree of life and live forever. So the Lord God sent him out of the Garden of Eden and made him cultivate the soil from which he had been formed. Then at the east side of the garden He put a living creature with a flaming sword which turned in all directions to prevent man from coming back."*

God's purpose from the beginning was for man to rule the world. God did not create man to die but to live forever, so long as he did not have the knowledge of good and evil. This is to make man less superior than his creator. If man had eaten both fruits, then we would all be like gods. To prevent this from happening, God had to chase man out of the Garden of Eden. God cursed them so that they could die physically but not spiritually, since He put his own life into man. The flesh has to go back to the soil, but the soul has to go back to the creator.

God is a loving and caring Father. In Genesis 1:31: *"God looked at everything he had made, and he was very pleased."* Despite the fact that he cursed human beings, God felt mercy for them. Adam said that he was naked, and therefore God made the first clothes out of animal skins for both of them. God treated them with kindness and love despite the fact that they had committed sins. They had run short of God's glory but not His love.

Later, the Garden of Eden was taken away from the face of the earth to heaven. Those who will make it to heaven will be allowed to eat fruits from the tree of life, for they will live forever. Those who will not shall die a second death because God will forget them forever. That is the second death. The Lord God shall forget them, and they will be thrown into the lake of fire forever.

When Moses asked God His name, he said, "I AM who I AM." In the Bible, the Lord God is in singular but not plural. This means that there is only one Lord God, Jehovah God, who is worthy to be praised and worshipped. The first three commandments protect God's supremacy. In Exodus 20:3–7, He said, *"I am the Lord your God who brought you out of Egypt, where you were slaves. Worship no other god but me. Do not make for yourselves images of anything in heaven or on earth or in the water under the earth. Do not bow down to any idol or worship it, because I am the Lord your God and tolerate no rivals. I bring punishment on those who hate me and on their descendants down to the third and fourth generation. But I show my love to thousands of generations of those who love me and obey my laws."*

In Deuteronomy 6:4–5, Moses said to the Israelites, "*The Lord and the Lord alone is our God. Love the Lord your God with all your heart, with all your soul and with all your strength.* In Deuteronomy 7:9–11, Moses reminded the Israelites that, "*The Lord your God is the only God and that he is faithful.*

During the temptation of Jesus, the Devil wanted to trap Jesus in order to worship other gods, so that God could be angry with him and then run short of God's glory. The three temptations were meant to do the same thing. In Luke 4:1–13, Jesus returned from Jordan full of the Holy Spirit and was led by the Spirit into the desert, where he was tempted by the Devil for forty days. In all that time, he ate nothing, so that he was hungry when it was over. The Devil said to Jesus, "*If you are God's son, order this stone to turn into bread,*" but Jesus answered, "*The scripture says, 'Man cannot live on bread alone.'*" Then the Devil took him up and showed him in a second temptation, all the kingdoms of the world. "*I will give you all this power and all this wealth,*" the Devil told Jesus. "*It has all been handed over to me, and I can give it to anyone I choose. All this will be yours, then, if you worship me.*" Jesus answered, "*The scripture says, 'Worship the Lord your God and serve only him.'*" Then the Devil took him to Jerusalem and set Jesus on the highest point of the Temple, and said to him, "*If you are God's Son, throw yourself down from here. For the scripture says, 'God will order his angels to take good care of you. It also says, 'They will hold you up with their hands so that not even your feet will be hurt on the stones.'*" But Jesus answered, "*The scripture says, 'Do not put the Lord your God to the test.'*" When the Devil finished tempting Jesus in every way, he left him for a while.

In the first and the third temptations, the Devil wanted Jesus to prove that he was the Son of God. This is great evidence that Jesus was the Son of God because the Devil acknowledged it. Love comes with trust.

If Jesus had turned stones to bread, then this would have meant that he did not trust God's word that man would not live by bread alone but by the word that comes from the mouth of God. Do not ask because others told you or you have seen others receiving, ask because you have a need.

The second temptation was very interesting because the Devil gave testimonies of how he possessed the world. The Devil acknowledged God and the fact that He is the creator of everything. He said he was given the earthly kingdoms though he did not mentioned who gave him; it was obvious he meant God, the creator. But when was this given? In the time when man fell short of God's glory. There was no one to rule the world because man was, at that time, on his own, working hard to get bread. The Lord God was no longer present for this world. This means that God took his Holy Spirit (Glory) away, and the whole world became dark. That is why Jesus said he is the light of the world.

God said that Jesus would be called Immanuel, which means, "God with us" or the glory of God back to the world again. That is why Jesus did not argue with the Devil, because the Devil had already dominated the world. The world was under God's curse and therefore it was not worthy in the eyes of the Lord God. In other words, the Devil took the world, which was garbage in the eyes of the Lord. In this connection, Jesus was not interested in garbage; he was interested in saving the golden ring, which is you and me who were in the garbage. That is why Jesus said, in Luke 12:33–34, *"Sell all your belongings and give the money to the poor. Provide for yourselves purses that do not wear out, and save your riches in heaven, where they will never decrease, because no thief can get to them, and no moth can destroy them. For your heart will always be where your riches are."* Your heart is the golden ring that Jesus came to save.

Jesus knew that earthly riches would blind human beings or would become obstacles to reaching God. This is because the Devil uses these riches so that man will forget God. This is a tool that the Devil uses for man to anger God because man would not love God with all his heart and mind.

The Devil tempted Jesus in three ways in order to break the three commandments of God. Each temptation represented a commandment of God. But the Christians of today are totally confused, including the preachers. They do not know when they are being tempted. That is why you find them promising greater miracles in order to prove they are true followers of Christ. But are they following in the footsteps of Jesus? Why do church ministers filled with the Holy Ghost stand on platforms and compete, deciding who can perform greater miracles? Does Jesus set such an example? To whom are they subject? They forget that whoever makes himself great will be humbled, and those who humble themselves will be made great. That is why Jesus was born poor, lived a poor life, and died a poor death. In Luke 9:57–58, a man said to Jesus, *"I will follow you wherever you go."* Jesus said to him, *"Foxes have holes, and birds have nests, but the Son of Man has nowhere to lie down and rest."* Actually, his disciples used to host him; other times, he would spend the night on the mountain, praying.

In Matthew 22:37, when Jesus was asked which is the greatest commandment, he answered, *"Love the Lord your God with all your heart, with all your soul, and with all your mind. This is the greatest and the most important commandment."* This means there is only one God, to be loved and worshiped, the creator of the universe and the Father of all.

God has seven spirits. Revelation 5:6: "*Then I saw a lamb standing in the center of the throne, surrounded by the four living creatures and the elders. The lamb appeared to have been killed. It had seven horns and seven eyes, which are the seven spirits of God that have been sent throughout the whole earth.* 1 Samuel 18:10–11: "*The next day an evil spirit from God suddenly took control of Saul, and he raved in his house like a madman. David was playing the harp, as he did every day, and Saul was holding a spear. 'I'll pin David to the wall,' Saul said to himself, and he threw the spear at him twice; but David dodged each time.*" In 1 Kings 22:19–22, Micaiah went on to say: "*Now listen to what the Lord says! I saw the Lord sitting on His throne in heaven, with all His angels standing beside Him. The Lord asked, 'Who will deceive Ahab so that he will go and be killed at Ramoth?' Some of the angels said one thing, and others said something else, until a spirit stepped forward, approached the Lord, and said, 'I will deceive him.' 'How?' the Lord asked. The spirit replied, 'I will go and make all Ahab's prophets tell lies.' The Lord said, 'Go and deceive him, you will succeed.'*" Whoever has wisdom will know the relationship between the other (man's) commandments and those spirits.

Not everyone will see God. Though he will be in that bright city, His Holy Place is hidden. There is only one door to enter into and one exit. But all in that city will feel His glory.

CHAPTER 30

CURSES

God used just a word to create the universe and its inheritance. His word has the power to destroy and to build. His word had an ability to create different species (inheritance) on earth without mentioning them one at a time. This includes all the wonderful things we can see and all of the things that we cannot see. The Bible tells us that God took six days to create the universe and its inheritance, but we do not know how long He took to create each kind of living and non-living thing. All we know is that God said let there be the sea and mainland, and at once the sea bore every kind of creature that can be found in the sea and the mainland.

When Adam and Eve ate the forbidden fruit in the Garden of Eden, God became angry with them. Anger is painful because it hurts. During the time of creation, God pronounced a blessing on everything that He created. This time, He was angry. He cursed them all. The words that he uttered had the power to destroy because they were alive. The words became like a spirit. It began to spread right from where He was, like a mist, to the whole world through the surface of the earth and up from the sea. The whole world and its inheritance was covered with this mist, which included the first parents who were created from the dust from the ground. It affects the souls of mankind. The mist leaves wounds and blisters on the soul and sometimes affects the brain, tormenting the person to death.

The whole world became an abomination to God because it became unclean. Something else that God had no intention of creating was born out of God's will—sin. This was meant to cause death also to all living things. The world experienced the absence of God. This means that God withdrew His presence and glory in this world, which was replaced with darkness. Love attracts but hatred repels, and therefore the peace and joy that comes from God were withdrawn also from the face of mankind. The mist can cover anyone, and once you are covered, no matter what you do to people, they will still dislike you and mistreat you. Wherever someone goes, they will become an outcast. It causes fear. All the blessings that are meant for him pass him by. This can cause anguish and misery in the heart.

The same mist causes poverty, disease, blindness, torment, lack of control, and rioting. The soul becomes like a rotten potato or rusted iron bar. When Miriam (Moses' sister) made God angry, she was covered by a mist that left her suffering from leprosy. It confines someone in a cocoon, where he or she remains lonely and unloved. Because of jealousy, Cain was tormented by the same curse that led him to kill his brother, Abel, and even to insult God himself.

One of the reasons for Jesus to come to this world was to partake in the curses of man and to break all the powers that they had. God gave him the power and authority to do so. He used words to make sons and daughters of men clean or holy again. He made the blind to see, healed those who were suffering from leprosy, made the lame walk again, and even brought back to life those who were dead.

Jesus became a victim of God's curse by being hated and isolated by people, though God was on His side. No one seemed to understand Him. Although he taught righteousness and love, he was not spared by this curse. He had to become a victim of this curse to be able to break it and destroy it. This is because a curse is a powerful tool of the Devil. It leads one to become fearful and desperate in life. Everyone turned against Jesus. They planned to eliminate him from this world. When Jesus died and was resurrected, the power of this original curse was broken and defeated.

The curse started from one point where God was standing and spread all over the world.

The blood that came from Jesus' limbs dripped onto the ground, breaking the curses right from the Calvary where the cross was planted to the ground. It then spread like fire and broke all over the world and under the world to the sea. The world that was once covered by curses was again covered with glory and the blessings of God through the blood of Jesus.

The blood of Jesus has the power to heal all wounds and remove the stains on our souls. All those who are covered by it are well-protected because it forms a shield. Whomever the blood of Jesus has washed, his soul is made clean and holy again indeed.

CHAPTER 31

GOD'S ANGER

One time the Holy Spirit of God took control of me. I was taken to heaven where on my way, I met with people running away to hide. I could feel a strong wind coming from the direction in which I was heading. I asked them why they were running, but they told me that they were running away from the anger of God. I joined them, and we ran away to a hiding place. Where I went to hide, I was in between two gentlemen who looked mighty, and I was very tiny compared with them. I looked at their faces, and I was surprised because I recognized them instantly. They were Moses and Elijah. I called them by their names. "Elijah, Moses why are you hiding?" They said to me, "Charles, when God is angry, no one can dare stay near him. You see the strong wind coming from His throne? No one can stand it. We have to hide and go back once He calms down."

Then I started walking towards the direction of the wind, but it was very strong. It was so strong that it was pushing me back. Then I called, "My Father, this is Charles, your love, your flower. You are angry, but you should look at me, your flower. Please stop being angry. I am coming to you." The wind began to soften. Then I heard the voice asking me, "Charles, you mean you do not fear me?"

"No," I replied. "I do not fear you. You are my Father, and I am your child. If you turn to fire, I will turn to fire, too, because I have your Holy Spirit and fire cannot consume fire."

Arguing with God

God has taught me about the Bible through reading and repeating in my dreams or visions the events that took place from Genesis to Revelation whenever I desired to experience the same. One of the most interesting ones was about Moses when God wanted to kill him in a tent. He was on his way to Egypt to carry out God's mission when God wanted to kill him and his wife saved him. I could not understand why God wanted to kill Moses, yet he was in God's mission and therefore I asked Him to explain the reason. Some few days later, I had this vision: I saw heaven open, and I saw a chariot descending towards me. It stopped where I was, and God told me to board because He wanted to teach me how to drive it. He showed me the buttons to press, and I drove it, though I was scared to death. It was moving at an unimaginable speed, the speed of light. I could imagine hitting an object or worse.

God told me to land the chariot along the coastline. We found two women who were dead, and He introduced them to me. He said to me, "Charles, this woman on the right was a born-again Christian, and the one on the left was not. Charles, if I may ask you, between the two women, whom do you want me to restore to life?" Of course, it was a matter of common sense. I replied, "The one who was a born-again Christian." Then He asked me to explain why I thought she deserved to live again. I said, "Well, because she knows you, she is saved, and she has been doing according to your will. She is your child." He commanded me to prophecy to the one who was not saved to come back to life. I said, "No, I should prophecy to the one who is saved." He commanded three times,

but I continued to say no.

Finally, He told me to board the chariot, leaving the women dead, and we took off. As I was controlling the chariot, He disappeared, and I was left alone. A few moments later, He appeared to me from the back seat. He held my hands at the back so that I could no longer control the chariot and my legs became stiff pressing the accelerator at the maximum. He told me, "Charles, I want to kill you now. I am going to cause you to crash with this chariot right now, and you will be no more." I asked Him, "Why, Lord? Why do you want to kill me? Are we not friends? Am I not your child?" He said to me, "Charles, because you argued with me. I introduced the two women to you but you did not know them. You have judged them by the little information that I gave to you. I created them, and I know their hearts and deeds. I judge people by their hearts, not by what they are claiming to be or by their appearance."

This time, I knew He had meant to kill me, and I pleaded with Him for forgiveness. "I am sorry, Father," I told him. He accepted my sincere repentance and spared my life, but He said, "Charles, arguing with me was the reason why I wanted to kill Moses. What I need is obedience and humbleness. My ways are not your ways. Nothing is impossible in my eyes, and nothing can be hidden from me. Do not ever argue with me because when you argue, you become an obstacle instead of an instrument to me." I went back to my dirty and rotten body, fitted into it, and immediately woke up.

God Was Angry With Me

One time I was at home in upcountry. On Sunday morning, God gave me a message to give to the congregation of the church that I was attending, St. John Thunguri Orthodox Church, in Mukurwe-ini. I left Mom at home, and I thought she was not coming for service. I never wanted to preach or sing in her presence because I feared her. I do not know why I feared her, because Mom was a committed Christian who used to encourage us to participate in church activities.

Before I asked to be given a chance to greet the congregation, my Mom came into the church. When I saw her, I declared that I was not ready to deliver the message. After the service was over, I went home and later went back to Nairobi in the afternoon. God never commented on anything.

After a week, I went to the mountain, Ngong Hill, to pray. I met with other people who had come to pray, too. We agreed to pray together first, and then we dispersed to pray on our own. One of the ladies, as she was leading the prayer, was touched by the Holy Spirit of God and said, "Charles, whom do you want to follow? Do you want to follow your mom or me? If your mom is an obstacle between you and me, then I will eliminate her. I cannot stand anyone between you and me." To my surprise, that lady had no idea what she meant or why she had spoken. I thought it was a secret between God and me. I repented my sins and since then I promised myself that I would always deliver God's messages without fearing anyone.

God Being Extremely Busy

One time, the sons of God were passing through the throne of God in order to take Him their harvest or the sacrifices that they had. The

Holy Spirit of God took control of me, and I found myself queuing along with the sons of God. I had fallen sick three days earlier, and my chest was hurting me. I took him a lamb that was pure white in color (I do not know where I got it from).

My turn came to give my sacrifice, and I handed over my lamb to Him. I stood there and He asked me, "Charles, what do you want?" I said, "I want you to touch my chest so that I can be healed." He said to me, "No, Charles. I am extremely busy. Cannot you see that all these people are waiting for me to serve them? Go and wait for me. I will come to heal you after this."

I replied to Him, "No, my Father. I do not want you to touch me, but just say a word and I will be healed. If you do not, I am not going to move." He looked at me, smiled, and touched my chest, and instantly the pain ceased. When I woke up, I had no pain.

Girlfriend

Before I moved to Nairobi, I had a girlfriend. With her, I had made the usual promises that we never fulfill. Our relationship was not all that close because of the problems that I was going through, and I thought no one cared or loved me. Early in 1990, when I started developing a good relationship with God, God appeared to me in a dream and instructed me to go home and break those promises because she would not be my wife. For now, I had to concentrate on nothing else except building my relationship with God.

I went home on a Friday and met her on Saturday. We agreed to meet again on Sunday afternoon. On Sunday afternoon, I met with her and after a long, general discussion, I asked her to tell me about her stand in our relationship. She told me that she had not changed her stand unless I was willing to do so. I did not want to break our relationship either. So, I went back to Nairobi in the evening without fulfilling God's will. I asked God to interfere because I did not want to break her heart.

Later, she came to Nairobi after a couple of months, but I did not know. One early morning, I met with her unexpectedly. We were happy to see each other and agreed to meet. We met twice, and later God revealed to me that she was moving out with a man she was working with. I asked her, but she said he was just a friend. I therefore broke my promises and set her free. That is the time God revealed to me that making promises to one another is wrong, but we should trust God to give us the best and his will be done.

God Does Not Force

God does not force us to make decisions or to do things that we cannot understand, but He does guide us and help us to understand which decisions are the best. He is not a dictator.

In the early 1991, I met a certain girl in Nairobi. I developed strong feelings towards her and even started going to see her at her office. After about two months, God sent someone to tell me to stop that relationship because it was not going to mature, and it was not His will. I confessed to the person who gave me the message that it was true.

When I went home, I had to pray, *God, will you please explain to me why I should leave that girl? I believe we are all your children. I know she is not saved, but you can change her heart. I have fallen in love with her, and I am not willing to let her go.*

That night I had a dream. In my dream, I was walking along a road when I reached a junction. There were two roads branching from the road upon which I was walking. After reaching the junction, I saw one road leading into darkness and the other one leading into a bright light. I heard a voice telling me to turn left, but I insisted that I must turn right, to the road that was leading to the darkness. I went ahead and I found the lady, the one God was telling me to leave. She was in darkness, but I went to her running, excited to see her. She was crying, and human feces surrounded her. I hugged her but there was nowhere to stand because of the human feces.

Then I looked straight across, and I could see the other road that I had refused to follow. In the middle of that road there was a very beautiful, slim, brown, medium-sized girl wearing a red dress. She had a smiling face and was surrounded by a ring of light. The beauty and glory that she had was beyond my imagination

Then I heard a voice asking me again, "Charles, between these two girls, whom would you take? The choice is yours. I wanted to give you the best, but if you do not want it, I cannot force you. But do not bother me in the future saying that you want me to change the one you have chosen because I have revealed to you why I told you to leave her. Do not be like other people who go to the church and once they find a lady or man who has a good voice or who is good-looking, then they start praying and fasting for me to unite them. You mortal men do not want to care about what will happen tomorrow. Today someone can be saved and tomorrow they can backslide. Someone may have good health today but will be ailing or dead tomorrow. I am the only one who knows about the future. Leave the matter to me; I will choose someone who will fit in your life."

Before he finished talking, I was on my way running towards the lady who was in the light, shouting with a loud voice, "I want the lady in the light. I want the lady in the light."

Forgetting God's Will

When I came to the United States, I did not know which church to attend or how to pray constantly the way I used to pray. I became spiritually weak and started fearing. As soon as I left Kenya, my niece had burned all my documents (the scripts) where I had recorded everything that God had revealed to me. Then the enemy thought that he had succeeded with his mission. I was tormented with the spirit of forgetfulness so that I could not recall anything that God had revealed to me. This spirit tormented me any time I thought of writing a book or doing my exams in class. It would affect me in the morning if the exams were in the afternoon and release me after the exams or when I went to sleep. I tried to pray, but I was too weak to have a breakthrough. God never used to talk to me. I lost all the power of dreams and visions and that devastated me. I became like an outcast, inhibited by the spirit of fear and forgetfulness.

After about one year, I met a new friend, Frank, who invited me to his church, the International Family Church, Winchester, MA. On Saturday night, I saw the church, the congregation, and the Pastor in my dream, and I was told to get my message there. When I woke up, I could tell how the preacher would be dressed and could recognize the lady who had a message for me.

The next morning, I went with Frank to the church. When people started praising and worshipping, I felt the presence of the Lord and immediately the Holy Spirit of God took control of the lady. She began to say, "You are my servant. Forget about your own home. This is your new home. I will make it comfortable for you. I made your ship turn around, as it was not moving forward. From now on, I have set it on a new course. I will be with you. You are the one I have chosen to talk to my people. Do not fear because I have been with you, and I will be with you. I am your God. Teach my people what I have taught you."

Those words really built me back up because I had lost hope, and I was desperate for contact with God, my best friend and my caring and loving Father. I was spiritually hungry but I'd had no food, and thirsty but with no water. I was lost in the desert. I did not hear what the preacher said on that day because I had received my message directly from God. All that I wanted to hear was the assurance that God was still with me and understood the pain I was going through. There was no one to tell me that he loved and cared for me. It was hard to live on my own without God.

Then I started gaining strength and hope. A few months later, we attended a prayer session in one of the Boston churches in the evening, and there was a lady who was preaching. I had met her before in my dreams. Because we were not many, we were greeting her in turn after the service was over. When it was my turn, she looked at me and said, "I do not know you, but God has chosen and anointed you to pass His message to the people. But why do you shy off doing God's will?" I replied to her that it was because I feared people. Then she said, "Charles, go and do what God sent you to do."

Then I had been wondering how to approach the issue because I knew what God had sent me to do, but how to do it was a problem. At that time, I could not recall those messages, and I did not want to write my own things. It was early in the year 2004 when someone appeared in my dream. He said, "Charles, I am your God. I have come to restore your memory regarding the messages and teaching that I used to give to you. Even though the documents where you had written my messages were destroyed, they are still saved somewhere as a treasure. Follow me, and I will show you the treasure. There is a book that contains all the information regarding the world, and it is hidden in a certain mountain."

We reached a place where there was big stone and a big tree, but the area was deserted. He said to me, "Charles, touch this stone and say the words 'earth, open in the name of Jesus,' three times."

I repeated these words, and the third time, the stone opened. There was a huge book lying underneath. It was very beautiful and clean, though covered with soil, and the tree had grown on top of it. He took it and held it in His hands. It became small in size, and then He rolled it like a chapatti before handing it to me. He said, "Charles, eat this book. It contains all the information that has been hidden since the time of creation. From today henceforth, the word of God has become a part of you. You will never forget again."

I took it and put it in my mouth. I chewed it and swallowed it. Since then, I started recalling all the things God used to reveal to me. Then after that, I started writing this book.

God Laughed at Me

One time, as I was pursuing an Advanced Diploma in Computer Studies, I deposited my school fees in one of the bank accounts that offered interest. It was in the beginning of the month, and therefore I was to go to withdraw money for school fees after my classes at midday. When I arrived, I found a commotion at the bank, and at first I could not understand what was happening. I joined the queue and at 1 p.m., the manager came out to address the customers. He told us that he had received instructions from the Central Bank of Kenya to close down until further notice because the bank was under liquidation. I could not understand what to do next, as I had no other source of money for school fees. I went home desperate and confused. I prayed to God for guidance, since He is the source of my strength and the only hope that I had.

The next morning, I went to school and explained to the principal what had happened. She granted me three weeks to sort out my financial problems. I tried consulting all the friends and relatives that I knew, but none had money to bail me out. I reached a point where I felt like giving up because I was in the middle of a desert. That night, I *did* give it up. I had a beautiful dream. In my dream, I saw heaven open, and I saw God seated on His throne. Then He watched me looking for money. What surprised me was that any time I approached an open door, He would order it to be closed. As I walked about, blindly, He laughed at me. The whole heaven kept silent because it was very unusual for God to laugh. I looked at heaven desperately and then He called out to me, "Charles, why are you disturbed and confused? Do not you believe and trust in me? Now go, and I have opened the door for you. Tomorrow you will get the money."

The next day I heard from the TV and radio that the clients of Trade Bank were to go and collect their funds. After two days, I went to collect my check, and I gave glory and honor to the king of kings. It was the first time I'd heard God laughing, and I have never heard it since.

I Laughed at Him, Stupidly

One day, I had a problem. I did not bother to pray about it. Instead, stupidly, I laughed at the Lord. Not only did I laugh at Him, but I also uttered a stupid comment. I said, "Lord, I am your child. My problem is your problem, and my victory is your victory. I know the battle is not mine but yours. Now, it is not I who is trapped in problems, but you. Let me sit aside and see how you are going to solve the problem." The way I said it was mocking, especially the last sentence. God was not happy about my behavior and comment, but He is a loving God. He solved the problem, but I cried because the solution was not a blessing; instead, it came with more problems. Since then, I have learned how to humble myself before God, to follow Him, and to let Him guide me instead of mocking Him.

Someone Prophesied Her Death

About ten years back, a lady I used to know had a dream. In her dream, she saw her own death, including her funeral. The dream was repeated about three times on different occasions. She became worried and asked me to pray for her.

I went back home and prayed for her. I received a shocking message. The message was, "Charles, go and tell her she is going to die. It's not someone else's death but her own she sees." I went and told her the message, but I thought it was a joke. She didn't believe either because she couldn't understand how God could allow her to die. Actually, she was asking, "Charles, do you think God could allow me to die?" In fact, I didn't take it seriously.

Unfortunately, she died about three years ago. I couldn't believe it when I learned of her death. Since then, I have come to understand that God is a loving God, but on the other hand, death is a must for all of us. Death does not mean that God does not love us. We should be grateful and wait for it patiently. We must recognize that one day we will die, whether we walk with the Lord or not. Therefore, we need to prepare ourselves each and every day to welcome it in our life. We should not fight it but embrace it.

CHAPTER 32

THE GRACE OF GOD

All human beings are sinners. We inherited sin while still in the womb of our mothers. Those are the sins committed by our first parents and also our forefathers. The curse that was pronounced by God to our first parents in the Garden of Eden follows us from the womb to the tomb. We try to avoid sins and walk in a righteous way, but we always find ourselves trapped in sin. Sins are like oceans or floods that cover the land, and therefore we cannot run from sin. We cling to the Lord to help us remain pure by walking carefully, but of course there are those who do not care. This is so because the fruit that Adam and Eve ate was the fruit of knowledge—to know what is good and what is bad.

Knowledge is a powerful, driving force. Man is an ambitious creature. Hence, curiosity can lead people astray. As a result, God gave Moses the Ten Commandments to guide mankind to be able to walk in the right way. Initially, man knew only how to do good things. God had put him in the path of righteousness, to walk along the path without getting confused. They did not understand evil because they were not knowledgeable about it. They were free to move anywhere in the Garden of Eden without fear. After they committed sin, God introduced limitations, and their power of freedom was reduced. They were put in chains or became slaves in order to follow the right path.

The chains were the Ten Commandments because that was the only way they could remain righteous, since they were in the desert.

When the Israelites were in the land of Egypt for 450 years, they were oppressed and tortured. Before they became slaves, they were free and had no limitations whatsoever in Egypt. They were put in chains as a sign of slavery, and all their rights deprived. No matter how hard they tried to please their masters, the masters could only see the mistakes they were making. As a result, they were punished, whipped, and ruthlessly killed. There were no rewards for them, as they had no rights.

God heard their cries and saw their suffering. He remembered the promises that He made with Abraham, and He was deeply touched in His heart. He promised to deliver them from the hands of evil men who were ready to destroy and to kill them. God sent Moses to set the Israelites free and to lead them to a free land. During that time, God taught them about Himself through Moses. This time they could see and feel the presence of the living God of their forefathers.

Though God had put them on the righteous path to follow freely, the knowledge they had gained from Egypt abhorred them from the righteous path. This made God angry because they rejected His teachings and the righteous path; instead, they decided to follow the knowledge that they had acquired from Egypt. This brought destruction upon them.

God is love and He is merciful. He delivered the Israelites from the hands of their oppressors because He loved their forefathers. There was no price to pay after deliverance. God wanted to see mortal man walking in the path of righteousness, freely and willingly. He decided to put chains on mortal man in order to be in control because man, on his own, could not do well. He wrote and gave Moses the Ten Commandments to be observed by man in order to remain in the path of righteousness. He wanted to draw them back to Him, not to control them but to serve and set them free with love and kindness.

When Moses was at Mount Sinai to receive the Ten Commandments for forty days, the people of Israel grew impatient. They decided to deviate from the will of God and to discover their own path to follow. God revealed to Moses what was going on with his people. At that time, God was angry with them and wanted to destroy them all. But Moses, being a good shepherd and a leader, pleaded with God to forgive them. He took their sins and asked God to spare them but to punish him instead, even if it meant his death. God honored Moses' request and spared the lives of the Israelites.

However, when Moses came down from the mountain, he saw, in reality, how the Israelites had become unfaithful. He became angry. Being controlled by anger, he threw the tablets holding the Ten Commandments onto the golden calf that had been made to be a god. He ordered the faithful people to be on one side and led the unfaithful to the other side. He ordered the faithful ones to kill the unfaithful ones. God was not pleased with Moses' act because when God had been angry, Moses had demanded that He forgive the Israelites. On the other hand, Moses was unable to forgive them. God does not pass judgment on any mortal man; instead, we judge ourselves and then we blame God. Moses had asked God to kill if He could not forgive the Israelites. Therefore, having judged himself, God had to kill Moses. That is why God told Moses that he would never step on the Promised Land; rather, he showed him the land because he loved him. Moses brought death upon himself, and maybe he could have ascended to heaven.

God loved man so much despite his wicked ways. He was the first to make clothes for Adam and Eve after they realized that they were naked. Though He was angry for their evil deeds, He was merciful to them. God's love is unconditional, and His grace is sufficient to all. He sent Jesus to come and die in order to reconcile man with God again. God offered salvation to mankind so that whoever is ready to accept it shall be saved. The decision is ours, but God has done everything possible to bring us back to His kingdom.

CHAPTER 33

WHAT IS FORGIVEN

One time I asked God to explain to me how sins will be remembered on the last day. Then it happened that as I was half-asleep, the heavens opened, and I saw a very huge store that looked to me like a library. The Spirit of God took control of me and took me inside of it. There was an angel at the door who asked me to identify myself. I said, "Jesus is the Lord. My name is Charles, the child of the Most High God." Then he looked at me and said, "Oh, you are Charles, I have heard about you. Come straight in." I went in and found many locked cabinets. I asked him to explain what was in those cabinets. He opened some of them and showed me some files. At first, they did not make sense to me, but after a while, he opened a drawer that had one of my sister's files. The file was huge, and in fact, a second one was being prepared.

The file was handed to me, and I started turning the pages. I could read each and every thing that she had done since her childhood. I could not understand why her file was still full, yet she was a born-again and a committed Christian. Actually, she became saved before I met Jesus. I asked the angel to explain to me why after getting saved, her case was still pending.

He looked at me and smiled. Then he asked me, "Charles, who told you that your sister was a born-again Christian?" I answered, "Even before I knew Jesus, before I was appointed to be a watchman in the house of the Lord, she was a committed Christian, going to church and giving testimonies." He said, "Oh, Charles, you mortal men have problems. Your sister is not saved because she wanted God to forgive her sins. As many of you have done, you do not seek God to forgive your sins; rather, you have personal needs that you want met—miracles from God. Coming to God for miracles or material things is one thing, and seeking God to forgive your sins and establish a good relationship with him is a different thing altogether. Your sister is committed because she fears that if she does not do so, her miracles will be taken away, like many of Christians today.

"Human beings believe that receiving miracles means forgiveness, but this is not true. Anyone can receive miracles from God so long as he or she is ready to receive. God is the creator of everything in the universe and does not discriminate against anyone. He releases blessings just the same way he releases rain or sunlight to all his creations. God knows every creature by name despite his or her iniquities. But a day is coming, a Day of Judgment, when the sinners and the righteous will be separated. Before that time comes, whoever calls upon the name of God shall be heard.

"Miracles are one of the tools the Devil uses to convince many of Christians that they are heading to heaven while they are going to hell. Those who are truly forgiven approach God with a humble and sincere heart, ready to receive a miracle of forgiveness of their sins. If you ask God for bread, you will get bread. If you ask for a fish, you get a fish. Those who ask God for material miracles refuse the miracle of salvation. A fish cannot be bread."

Then I asked him to explain to me how those files were recorded. He said to me, "We angels work to monitor human beings. Angels are assigned to a human being from the time of their birth in order to serve them. We protect, guide, and record every activity a man does. Nothing can go unrecorded because we are accurate. The brain is connected to a soul, and a soul is connected to a file. Whatever goes into a human mind is also recorded in soul, and hence automatically recorded on the person's file. That is how we are able to record everything without omission. If a human being receives a miracle of salvation then God commands that his or her file be destroyed, and his or her sins will be remembered no more. But there are others who do not have files, those who have a good relationship with God, so we do not need to protect or report them. God has their images drawn on his hand. He watches them just the same way you watch TV. So happy are those who have been made the children of the Most High God, because God is always watching them. When they sin, they are corrected with love, and no harm can fall on them. The angels have nothing to do with those who walk with God. They cannot be condemned by anyone because they are faithful and righteous in the eyes of God. This does not mean only Christians but any human being in the world who chooses to walk with God by trusting and doing what pleases God. It depends on the heart of the person."

Then, I looked at him and looked at the file. I asked him, "Sir, may I ask you for a favor?" He said, "Sure." I said, "Will you please destroy this file of my sister and prepare a new one for her?"

He smiled, looked at me, and then took the file. Then he said, "Charles, as a human being, you have power and authority from God that we angels do not have because God loves you. We are here to serve you. If you order me to destroy it, then it will be done." He opened the file, took all the papers out, and put them into a machine to be destroyed.

He took new plain papers and prepared a new file for my sister. Glory is to God on High.

Then, before I left, he told me, "Charles, you see all those files are pending cases for millions of people on earth. Churches are full of unborn Christians who claim every day that they are born again. They failed to seek God for forgiveness first. Therefore, go and tell everyone, especially Christians who claim to be born again, to seek miracles of forgiveness first. Tell them to repent their sins from deep within their hearts, not within their flesh. Commitments in the church out of fear of losing those miracles they have received do not make them better than those who do not know God. Forgiveness of sins is what matters to God. Forgiveness comes from God, and those God has forgiven have become His own children. Their images are drawn on His hand the moment they are forgiven. For miracles, God orders angels to release blessings to those who are asking for them without bothering to know who they are. God says, 'If they are interested in blessings, give them blessings to stop bothering me.' Then the Devil comes in praising because he has an opportunity to whisper to the miracle receivers. This is what the Devil says: "You see, there is no way you can receive miracles if God does not love you. Your sins are forgiven, and you can continue with your normal life because God loves you." But it is a lie. The Devil is aware that God does not even bother to know who asked for material blessings. You become blind and believe your sins are forgiven, but you will be surprised because your sins will be read from the first one to the last one you committed during your lifetime on earth." It is true that God loves us all, but we have run short of God's glory.

Forgiveness of sin is not a one-time thing. Every day you pray, remember to cleanse yourself before God. We do wrong things when conscious or unconscious of what we are doing. Even when we sleep the Devil steals our mind, and we commit sins during those times. Therefore, every morning when we wake up, and every evening before we retire to bed, we must cleanse ourselves by asking God for forgiveness because we do not know what the angels have recorded in our file that does not please God. The process of prayers should be Repentance, Praise, and Worshipping, and other things you may want to add. For instance, I always see myself naked in the eyes of the Lord day and night. Our thoughts and minds make us look naked, unrighteous and unholy in the eyes of the Lord, in spite of how hard we try to do good.

CHAPTER 34

DO NOT TEST GOD

Deuteronomy 6:16: *"Do not put the Lord your God to the test. Be sure that you obey all the laws that He has given you. Do what the Lord says is right and good, and all will be well with you."*

In the book of Isaiah 7:10–13, the king (Lord) sent another message to Ahaz: *"Ask your God to give you a sign. It can be from deep in the world of the dead or from high up in heaven." Ahaz answered, "I will not ask for a sign. I refuse to put the Lord to the test."*

We give because it is a blessing to give more than to receive. We do not trust or believe in God because He proves to us that He is God. We believe in God because He is the creator of everything, and He is the only one worthy to be praised and worshipped. With or without blessings, we need to give thanks to God for the basic things He has given to us—air that we breathe, good health, life, a vision for the future, and above all, salvation.

Let us accept the simple fact that we have no right to claim the kingdom of God. It is through His grace that He has blessed us with free salvation. We do not deserve to inherit or ask Him for anything because we do not live according to His perfection. But because of His kind heart, He extended His unconditional love to us. It is a privilege to be called the child of the Most High God, but not a right despite our religion, race, or color. We owe Him everything, including our lives, but He owes us nothing. Therefore, we need to be humble in His presence and give Him the respect that He deserves instead of beating our chests demanding blessings or putting God to the test.

Most Christians live a stressful life because they compare themselves with others. If you are not receiving from God, it does not mean that you are a sinner. God has a good plan for you. What is important is not how much you can receive but how much you can give in terms of time and commitment. You may have little because God wants to glorify himself. Let the will of God be done. Look upon Him and be satisfied. The love that God has for you is just enough for you to praise Him. He has provided you with security because your future is in His hands. It is a wonderful thing to receive His precious gifts. He protects you from the power of death, and His presence fills you with joy and peace. Do not be cheated by those who are lost so that you can be like them. You cannot serve two masters. They are blind, and want you to be blind, too.

Remember that righteousness will save you when the disaster strikes. When the day of the Lord comes, your material prosperity will not save you. In fact, these things will be the first things to perish. God has put you in the condition you are in today and has given you courage to persevere. Sing the songs of praise and worship Him without ceasing, and your reward shall be great. Earthly riches will not save you from going to the grave. Thankful, giving hearts do win and touch the heart of the Most High God.

Let us be like the prodigal son. He acknowledged his faults or sins. He made up his mind to go back to his father to repent and request that his father make him to be like one of his servants. He did not say that he had a right to inherit his father's property.

First, we must acknowledge our faults and sins deep within our hearts. Then we need to approach our Father with humility, seeking forgiveness because we have no rights, but we can gain God's favor back. God will welcome us back to His kingdom and give us the privileges of His kingdom. We must be careful not to abuse those privileges.

Therefore, it is not a question of what to receive but what to give back to God; not what God is going to do but what God has done for us and what we are going to do for Him; not what we can expect from God but what God expects from us.

CHAPTER 35

WHERE DOES GOD LIVE?

God has His holy place. Not even angels are allowed to enter there. The New Jerusalem is built around this Holy city. The angels and the saints live in heaven but God comes to visit them. That is why the Devil thought that he was very powerful and could overthrow God's kingdom. The archangel Michael went to God and informed Him of what was going on.

Not all of us will see God with our eyes. Only those who are pure in their hearts will be allowed to enter into the holy place to sit together with God at His table. Some of us will be in the city but will not have an opportunity to see God; we may only feel His presence. Others will be so poor that though they will be dressed in white, they will live outside the gates of the holy city.

Jesus said that in his Father's house there are many places, and he has gone to build mansions for you and me. God is hard-working and good in planning. He always communicates His plans and provides measurements, if necessary. Though the Bible tells us that God took seven days to create the universe, in the real sense, it was not the seven days of our normal week. According to the Bible, to God one day is equivalent to a thousand years. In short, we do not know how many years it took God to create the universe. It might be in terms of thousands or millions of years or more. We also do not know how long Adam lived without a helper.

According to the Bible, it took Noah about a hundred years to build the ark (boat). God commanded him to build it and gave him the measurements. God could have provided him with a ready-made boat, but God wanted to test Noah's faith and patience. It took forty days and nights for the flood to fill the earth. God was able to command the water to rise within a minute and to cover everything, but He did not. It took Jesus about thirty years while God was preparing him for His mission. While Jesus could have appeared from heaven and started his ministry from nowhere, it did not happen this way. It took Jesus forty days and forty nights in the wilderness waiting to be tempted by the Devil, but the Devil could have come on the first day. Abraham took more than ten years before receiving a promised son, while God could have fulfilled His promise immediately.

That is why it has taken Jesus many years to return, because he has to build mansions for us in the Holy City of God. It may take a couple of thousand years, but the fact is that the day the project is complete; Jesus will come back for us. It is true that where there is willingness, there is love and a plan.

In that city, there will be no mourning, crying, sadness, jealousy, angry, hunger, poverty, pain, or death. All those bad things that cause misery will not enter into the Holy city. The gates of that city will stand open all day; they will never be closed because there will be no night there, according to the book of Revelation 21, *The city will have no sun or the moon because the glory of God shines on it and the Lamb of God, Jesus the Christ will be the Lamp. The people of all nations of the world will walk by its light. But nothing that is impure will enter the city, nor any one who does shameful things or tells lies. The Holy City belongs only to those whose names are written in the Lamb's book of the living because the kingdom, honour and the glory belongs to God forever and ever Amen.*

According to the book of the Revelation 22, there will be the river of the water of life, sparkling like crystal. It will be flowing from the throne of God and of the Lam, down the middle of the city's street. On each side of the river there will be the tree of life, which bears fruit twelve times a year, once each month; and its leaves will be for the healing of the nations. Nothing that is under God's curse will be found in the city. That is why we need to be cleansed by the blood of the Lamb, Jesus Christ because it has power to break God's curse. How wonderful that will be! The beauty and glory in that Holy City never fades or dies, unlike our beauty. The kings of the earth will take their wealth into the Holy City. The kings are all those who have come out victorious, who have walked with God and have washed their garment by the precious blood of God. It is not the politicians, but anyone who has pleased God.

The streets of the city will be covered with God's glory. We talk about gold, silver, and diamonds, but more precious and valuable stones than those we know will be found in this beautiful Holy City.

Holy Place of God

One day I was sleeping, and the Holy Spirit of God took control of me. I saw heaven open and someone identified Himself as God walking with me in heaven. We reached two identical doors. He said to me, "Charles, do you see these doors?" I said, "Yes." He further explained the purpose of each door—that one door was an entrance and the other was an exit. He pointed to the door to enter and then to the door to exit. He then said to me, "Charles, there are no exceptions. You must be extremely cautious because whoever makes a mistake by confusing them dies." I became worried and asked Him, "Who then will help me identify them, in case I forget?" He looked at me and smiled. "Charles, Jesus will be there to help you, do not worry, he will teach you."

Those two doors led to the Holy Place of God. God has created heaven for angels and earth for man, but He has a special place where He lives. Even the angels are not allowed to enter into His Most Holy Place. That is where Jesus said he would go to prepare mansions for us in our Father's house. The New Jerusalem was to be built around the Most Holy Place of God.

These two doors were extremely beautiful and full of glory beyond imagination. That is why the Devil wanted to overthrow God's kingdom, because God does not live with angels in heaven but comes to visit them.

What surprised me was that it was hard to differentiate the right from the left because there is no directions there, no east or west or north or south. Then He led me out and told me that I had been given the authority to pass through the doors. Ezekiel 42:23–26 and 43:1–4 also explained these two doors.

This is true because according to the Bible in the book of Revelation 20.11, the Earth and Heaven shall flee from the presence of Jesus and will be seen no more. This is evidence that God does not reside in heaven but has His own Holy Place.

Who Will Enter into the Holy City of God?

Many people get confused about this issue of who will inherit the kingdom of God. There are many religions in the world, and each believes that they are the right one. When God called Abraham, He wanted his descendants to teach and to bless the rest of the world, not because they were righteous but because they had gained God's favor through their ancestors. They did not please God and instead did what pleased them. They did not walk in the right way God had prepared for them by meeting God's standards. As a result, many perished in the wilderness. God called them for blessings but instead they chose suffering and death. Only a few made it to the Promised Land. The majority of those who entered into the Promised Land were of a new generation, not those who were called from Egypt. Therefore, many were called from the land of suffering (Egypt), but few made it to the land of blessings, the Promised Land (Canaan). God wanted to demonstrate his existence and power to the world through the Israelites.

Jesus came to bring salvation to all mankind so that we could inherit the kingdom of God by showing us the right way to follow. God so loved the world that He gave us the precious gift of salvation so that whoever is ready to accept it, shall be saved. He has given us free will to choose what we feel is good for us. He does not force anyone to accept His salvation. The whole world has been invited to the kingdom of God through Jesus Christ but few have chosen to accept.

The citizenship of heaven is open to anyone who accepts this invitation through Jesus Christ. Those who reject this will not blame God because the choice is theirs. When our first parents rebelled against God, God felt merciful because of the suffering that was ahead of them. Therefore, God promised to bring them back to the Garden of Eden. That is why He chose Abraham in order to bless the whole world. He had to prepare a way of saving mankind from the slavery of his own sins. He wanted to reveal Himself to the whole world through miracles and great deeds. He also wanted to prepare the world for the future and how His knowledge would be passed from generation to generation. If Jesus was born without preparation, then he could not have been influential and His teaching would have been nothing more than a myth. But by the time he came, God had revealed Himself to the world through Moses and the other prophets.

Jesus' mission was only to strengthen what people knew about God. Therefore, the Israelites were not called to be the only heir of the kingdom of God but to prepare the way for the salvation of the world. The rest of the world should not feel inferior and conclude that God discriminated or isolated the rest of the world. He has a right to use anyone for His glory. We are all His children, and His love is unconditional to everyone; it is His blessings, or grace, or glory, or salvation that is conditional.

In the book of John, it says, *"For God loved the world so much that he gave his only Son so that everyone who believes in him may not die but have eternal life."* God's purpose to send Jesus into the world was to bring salvation to all mankind. Those who accepted Jesus have accepted God's salvation because they are standing in the promises of God. They are eligible to inherit the kingdom of God, to be citizens in the house of the Lord, the Holy City, and to be the royal family.

I respect all other religions because they teach about goodness against evil. I have no right to judge who is true and false. No one knows who will be worthy to go to heaven and who will go to hell except God Himself. But they need to accept God's gift to mankind, the forgiving of sins. Jesus was given the power and authority to judge the world after defeating the powers of darkness. It is only through his name that we may cast out or rebuke demons and other evil spirits. His name is a spiritual super-weapon we have to fight our spiritual enemies. Without Jesus, we have no spiritual victory because we lack a super-weapon. The Devil and his followers fear the blood of Jesus, the power of the cross, and Jesus' name above all names. Every knee shall bow before him and acknowledge him to be the king of kings, the Son of God, because he gained favor from above. Therefore, everyone has been invited into the Holy City despite our religious background because all of us have fallen short of God's glory and need salvation. We are all called to be heirs in the Holy City of God.

Those who have been called by His name have gained God's favor, and their names have been written in the book of life. Jesus went to the Holy Place of God to prepare a place for you and me, so that is where he is, and we can be, too. This means that those who are called by His name shall be given the first priority because they are the true citizens of the Holy City. But this does not mean that the rest will go to hell. As a matter of fact, only God can know who is to go to heaven and who is not. But through His son, Jesus Christ, is the easiest and most direct way. They will reign with Jesus a thousand years and forever more. Remember many are called, but few are chosen.

Psalm 15

Who may worship in the holy city, your sacred hill? A person who obeys God in everything and always does what is right. A person whose words are true and sincere, and who does not slander others.

He does no wrong to his friends and does not spread rumors about his neighbors. He despises those whom God rejects, but honors those who obey the Lord.

He always does what He promises, no matter how much it may cost. He makes loans without charging interest and cannot be bribed to testify against the innocent. Whoever does these things will always be secured and enter in the Holy City of God. According to Revelation 22.14, happy are those who wash their robes clean and so have the right to eat the fruit from the tree of life and to go through the gates into the Holy City.

CHAPTER 36

PRAYERS

Through prayers, we communicate with our God. We let Him know our needs and wants. We also express our appreciation and offer our sacrifices. But what prayers are productive? What prayers will be heard by God? What prayers touch the heart of God? In most cases, the prayers that we pray do not go directly to God. We have angels who serve us, and therefore, they usually take the prayers to the holy temple. The angels decide which prayers to present to God. That is why sometimes prayers take time to be answered and others are forgotten, especially if the prayer is a complaint. I saw angels who were ashamed to present a prayer request because the prayers were not well thought of.

The effective way to pray is through praise and worship, for then the gates of heaven open. God comes down to receive the sacrifices of praise and worship. He cannot send anyone else to receive these things. God created human beings also to worship and praise Him. God wanted His will to be done on earth, as it is always done in heaven. In heaven, there is no ministry of healing, preaching, counseling, pasturing, or praying. In heaven, there is only one ministry, the ministry of worshipping and praising God. The ministry of worshipping and praising was there before the creation of the world, and it is the only ministry that will be left after the end of the world. Therefore, my dear brother or sister, you cannot claim that you do not have a ministry. Actually, worshipping and praising are part of being human. That is your basic purpose in this world.

When you have needs to express to our almighty God, communicate through praises. If you form this habit of worship and praise, then you will be walking with God. He will reveal Himself to you, and the events that are ahead of you, including the traps and temptations of the Devil. God will be receiving your prayers directly because angels will have no authority regarding your prayers.

Therefore, if you have to pray, humble yourself and recognize that you are in the presence of the almighty God, the king of kings. Teach yourself good manners and believe that you are talking to God face-to-face. Show Him that you recognize and acknowledge His presence. If you have nothing to tell Him, just say our Lord's Prayer or give thanks. For example: *"I thank you God for the day or night, thank you for food, good health, and protection. I thank you for the air that we breathe, the rain that you send to the plants, the snow to beautify the world, and the sun we enjoy. Thank you for everything that you have created, and thank you for the day ahead of me. Be with me, protect me, let me do your will and see your glory. Lord, I will give you thanks in the evening and morning for being with me, in Jesus' name. Amen."*

When you pray or fast, do not do it for material prosperity and success; pray persistently for spiritual blessings and, in fact, the material blessings will be automatic. Do you know that there are millions of spiritual gifts that God has for you apart from the gifts and fruits of the Holy Spirit that are mentioned in the Bible? When will you ever receive them?

When you humble yourself before God, He will bless you with millions of spiritual gifts. He will draw your image on His Holy hand. He will be watching you throughout your life. He will clear the way for you and make a way where there was no way. You will realize that your life was in danger after being saved. You will be healed before you get sick. Your work will be praising and worshipping the king of kings. His presence will grant you power and authority from above. Your wishes will always come true before you even pray because God will bless your heart's desire when you are asleep. The blessings will be waiting for you, but not for you to wait for them. Prayers will be an asset for you because in times of danger, or when you cannot pray for yourself, God will remember your praises and worship, and then bless or rescue you.

When you pray, do not shout or yell, or fight the air, because you scare the angels. Remember, you are in the presence of the king of kings, the angels, and the holy of holies. Behave like a small child presenting a bouquet of flowers to a king. Learn how to approach the throne of God with respect and humility. It is true that God's kingdom is ours, but we must show Him that we are worthy in His eyes. It was through His grace that we are saved, not through our deeds, might, or power. The kingdom of God is for those who will humble themselves like children. God is simple, and His ways are simple, too. The kingdom of God is here with us through Jesus Christ. Let us praise and worship God.

In Matthew 6:5–13, Jesus told his disciples, "When you pray, do not use a lot of meaningless words, as the pagans do, who think that God will hear them because their prayers are long. Do not be like them. Your Father already knows what you need before you ask Him." This is how he taught his disciples to pray:

Our Father, who art in heaven,
Hallowed be thy Name.
Thy kingdom come.
Thy will be done,
On earth as it is in heaven.
Give us this day our daily bread.
And forgive us our trespasses,
As we forgive those who trespass against us.
And lead us not into temptation,
But deliver us from evil.
For thine is the kingdom,
and the power,
and the glory,
for ever and ever.
Amen.

Power of Prayer

Sometime back in December 1994, I wanted to understand the power of prayer. Therefore, I decided not to pray for some time. Then I was put into a cocoon because the Devil and his followers could not touch me, though they could build walls around me. After a few weeks, I could not have a breakthrough whenever I prayed. I could hear my voice out of the darkness, but could not see myself in the light, as I usually do. I was lost in the darkness and hidden by the Devil.

Then, on January 4, 1995, I met with a group of thugs (a gang) in Nairobi at 10 a.m. They robbed me of everything and tore my clothes. I was left nearly naked. I cried out with a loud voice, spiritually, and the walls of the cocoon broke into pieces that day. I had peace of mind, and I could see the light once again.

No one could see me when I was cocooned. The heavenly body could hear my voice but could not see me.

Thanksgiving Prayers

O God, you are my God, and I long for you. My whole being desires you; like a dry, worn-out, and waterless land, my soul is thirsty for you. Let me see you in the sanctuary; let me see how mighty and glorious you are. Your constant love is better than life itself, and so I will praise you. I will give thanks to you as long as I live; I will raise my hands to you in prayer. My soul will feast and be satisfied, and I will sing glad songs of praise to you.

As I lie in bed, I remember you; all night long I think of you, because you have always been my help. In the shadow of your wings, I sing for joy. I cling to you, and your hand keeps me safe. Those who are trying to kill me will go down into the world of the dead. They will be killed in battle, and their bodies eaten by wolves. Because God gives him victory, the king will rejoice. Those who make promises in God's name will praise Him, but the mouths of liars will be shut.

Psalm 25: Guidance and Forgiveness

To you, O Lord, I offer my prayer; in you, my God, I trust. Save me from the shame of defeat; do not let my enemies gloat over me! Defeat does not come to those who trust in you, but to those who are quick to rebel against you. Teach me your ways, O Lord; make them known to me. Teach me to live according to your truth, for you are my God, who saves me. I always trust in you. Remember, O Lord, your kindness and constant love, which you have shown from long ago. Forgive the sins and errors of my youth. In your constant love and goodness, remember me, Lord!

Because the Lord is righteous and good, He teaches sinners the path they should follow. He leads the humble in the right way and teaches them His will. With faithfulness and love, He leads all who keep His covenant and obey his commands. Keep your promise, Lord, and forgive my sins, for they are many. Those who obey the Lord will learn from Him the path they should follow. They will always be prosperous, and their children will possess the Holy City of God. The Lord is the friend of those who obey Him, and He affirms His covenant with them.

I look to the Lord for help at all times, and He rescues me from danger. Turn to me, Lord, and be merciful to me, because I am lonely and weak. Relieve me of my worries and save me from all my troubles. Consider my distress and suffering and forgive all my sins. See how many enemies I have; see how much they hate me. Protect me and save me; keep me from defeat. I come to you for safety. May my goodness and honesty preserve me, because I trust in you.

Psalm 32: Confession and Forgiveness

Happy are those whose sins are forgiven, whose wrongs are pardoned. Happy is the man whom the Lord does not accuse of doing wrong and who is free from all deceit. When I did not confess my sins, I was worn out from crying all day long. Day and night you punished me, Lord; my strength was completely drained, as moisture is dried up by the summer heat. Then I confessed my sins to you; I did not conceal my wrongdoings. I decided to confess them to you, and you forgave all my sins.

So all your loyal people should pray to you in times of need; when a great flood of trouble comes rushing in, it will not reach them. You are my hiding place; you will save me from trouble. I sing aloud of your salvation, because you protect me.

The Lord said to me, "I will teach you the way you should go; I will instruct you and advise you. Do not be stupid like a horse or a mule, which must be controlled with a bit and bridle to make it submit."

The wicked will have to suffer, but those who trust in the Lord are protected by His constant love. You that are righteous, be glad and rejoice because of what the Lord has done. You that obey him, shout for joy!

Psalm 30: Thanksgiving

I praise you, Lord, because you have saved me. I cried to you for help, O Lord my God, and you kept my enemies from gloating over me. I cried to you for help, O Lord my God, and you healed me; you kept me from the grave. I was on my way to the depths below, but you restored my life. Sing praise to the Lord, all his faithful people! Remember what the Holy One has done, and give Him thanks! His anger lasts only a moment, His goodness for a lifetime. Tears may flow in the night, but joy comes in the morning.

I felt secure and said to myself, "I will never be defeated." You were good to me, Lord; you protected me like a mountain fortress. But then you hid yourself from me, and I was afraid. I called to you, Lord; I begged for your help: "What will you gain from my death? What profit from my going to the grave? Are dead people able to praise you? Can they proclaim your unfailing goodness? Hear me, Lord, and be merciful! Help me, Lord!"

You have changed my sadness into a joyful dance; you have taken away my sorrow and surrounded me with joy. So I will sing praises to you. Lord, you are my God; I will give thanks to you forever.

Psalm 86: Prayer for Help

Listen to me, Lord, and answer me, for I am helpless and weak. Save me from death, because I am loyal to you; save me, for I am your servant and I trust in you. You are my God, so be merciful to me; I pray to you all day long. Make your servant glad, O Lord, because my prayers go up to you. You are good to us and forgiving, full of constant love for all who pray to you. Listen, Lord, to my prayer; hear my cries for help. I call to you in times of trouble, because you answer my prayers. There is no God like you, O Lord; no one has done what you have done. All nations that you have created will come and bow down to you; they will praise your greatness. You are mighty and do wonderful things; you alone are God.

Teach me, Lord, what you want me to do, and I will obey you faithfully; teach me to serve you with complete devotion. I will praise you with all my heart, O Lord my God; I will proclaim your greatness forever. How great is your constant love for me! You have saved me from the grave itself.

Proud men are coming against me, O God; a gang of cruel men are trying to kill me—people who pay no attention to you. But you, O Lord, are a merciful and loving God, always patient, always kind and faithful. Turn to me and have mercy on me; strengthen me and save me, because I serve you, just as my mother did. Show me proof of your goodness, Lord; those who hate me will be ashamed when they see that you have given me comfort and help.

Holy Communion

One night I was sleeping, and a glorious light appeared to me. Then someone appeared, and I could feel the presence of God. He called me by my name. "Charles! Let us go out." Then I left my body and accompanied Him. We stood outside the house, and I could see beautiful fruit trees. Then He asked me, "Charles, do you like that fruit?" All the trees had ripened fruit.

I told Him, "I like them very much, and I am thankful. Do you want some? I will pick some from the tree for you." He smiled at me and then said, "No, Charles. I made them for you because you are in the flesh. Your body needs food to grow and to remain strong. In spirit, you do not need food."

Then He looked straight into my eyes and asked me, "Charles, why do my people not honor Holy Communion? They prepare their own food, yet they cannot prepare Holy Communion." Then I said, "We buy bread and when we pray for God to bless the food, we believe God will change it to be the body and blood of Jesus."

He said, "Charles, it is not what you are taking but how you have prepared what you are taking. Jesus and his disciples used to take dinner, but the night he was to be betrayed, they prepared a special dinner. He ordered his disciples to go and prepare a table for supper. During suppertime, Jesus talked about his death and also took the water and washed his disciples' feet. This last supper prepared Jesus for the temptations that were ahead of him by giving him courage and strength, and allowed him to bid a farewell to his disciples. Washing their feet was a sign of humility and submission to the will of God. It is important that people honor Holy Communion."

Then I asked Him, "How can we honor communion?" He said, "Communion must be prepared in prayers. Communion is not just the regular food you pray for before eating. Communion heals, gives strength and courage. Communion must be prepared in seven stages or using seven different prayers. Gather all the ingredients and items to be used together."

Then at once we were in a kitchen, and He demonstrated these steps to me:

Step 1: Call all those who are around and pray for forgiveness of sins and cleansing. Ask forgiveness from one another.

Step 2: As you mix ingredients, or make dough, pray for God to change those ingredients into the body of Christ.

Step: 3: As you put the fire on, pray for the utensils to be used and ask God to add the fire of the Holy Spirit.

Step 4: Pray for God to bless or to enrich the bread with spiritual gifts such as healing, love, kindness, joy, peace, and the power to defeat evil.

Step: 5: Remove the bread from the fire and give thanks to the Lord; also pray for those who will take the communion—not just anybody but those God has chosen. Then store it nicely and safely.

Step 6: Before the service begins, those who were responsible for the preparation must go to where the communion is stored and pray. Give thanks to the Lord, bless the communion, and pray for those who are taking it.

Step 7: Pray for forgiveness and thanksgiving by all before taking the communion.

He gave me the communion to eat, but He did not eat. Then He told me to wait for Him because He was coming soon for me. I refused to be left and reached out for His robes. He looked at me and in an instant, He was gone. I was left holding nothing but disappointment because He did not take me with Him.

Honoring God While Praying

One time, yet again, the Holy Spirit took control of me, and I found myself in the presence of God. I could see Jesus standing at a distance, covering his head and looking sad. Then I heard a voice telling me, "Charles, welcome to my Holy Place."

I found myself in very beautiful surroundings, and I knew that someone was seated on a throne; His Light was very bright. I did not dare look at Him, and I seemed very tiny in His presence.

I became more concerned about Jesus and asked the One who was seated on the throne, "Father, why is Jesus so lonely and sad? He does not smile as I do, and why was he covering his head when he was praying?"

And the Father said to me, "Charles, Jesus is there, go and ask him those questions you are asking me."

I went straight to Jesus and stood next to him. I asked him, "Jesus, why are you covering your head?" He answered, "Charles, it is a sign of respect to God. God is the creator of the universe and everything in it. There is no one like Him. He deserves respect. Covering my head is a sign of submission to His will. I was sent by Him, and I want to do what pleases Him." Then he fell silent.

I looked at him and asked him, "But Jesus, why are you worried? You look sad and yet you have gained favor in the Holy City of God. You have defeated your enemies, and you were crowned to be the king of kings. Why then are you anxious? You are not as jolly as me, yet I am still only in my material form."

He looked at me and smiled. Then he said to me, "Charles, I have no reason to be happy at all. Look down there, into the world! My people are ignorant; they do not know where they are coming from or where they are going. My enemy and his followers know their destiny, but my people act as if they have no destiny."

"When I was in the world, my heart was in agony because of the temptations that were ahead of me. The pain that was waiting for me was too much. Though I did not know exactly what was waiting for me, my Father used to reveal it to me day by day. Today, I am a king in the house of God, yes, but when I see that the pain that I went through is the same pain waiting for those who reject me or for those who are not doing God's will, that is what makes me feel sad and worried."

"I cannot be a king in the house of the Lord without my people. I suffered so that anyone who believes in my Father and me can inherit the kingdom of God. But few are on the right path of salvation— millions are lost in the world. Those who have accepted me have joy and peace because eternal pain is not awaiting them. My happiness and joy will be fulfilled when I see multitudes of people heading to the Holy Place of God. A bridegroom cannot rejoice or be happy until he holds the hand of his bride heading home."

Then I left him without a word and went back to the throne of God.

I heard God's voice telling me, "Charles, if you want Jesus to be happy and to rejoice, then do my will. Be like him: humble yourself and do what pleases me. Also, teach my children how to humble themselves and to do my will."

Then I went back to my body and fitted myself in.

CHAPTER 37

DAY OF THE LORD

I asked God to explain what will happen and how people will be chosen to enter into the kingdom of God. I saw the end of the world and people were floating in the air because there was no earth and sky. Both the earth and the sky will fade away.

God said to Jeremiah, *"I knew you before you were formed in your mother's womb. I anointed you to be my prophet and therefore do not say that you are young, that you cannot go. The long journey of life in this merciless and bitter world starts from the womb and ends at the tomb. This is because death can come to those in their mother's womb or to those already born."*

The reason God creates a human being is to have him as His best friend and to be a ruler of the World. That is why He gave him physical form, because everything else in the world had a physical form.

Man is God's representative, and therefore he can make decisions independently because God gave him free will to choose what is good for him. The same purpose has not changed, though the Devil wanted to frustrate God's plan by separating man from the love of God.

When a child is formed in the womb, it marks the beginning of a long journey. There is a long road that connects the world and heaven, spiritually, but it has many exits along the way. This is a righteous highway designed by God. Those exits are all dead ends, but the angels are waiting with chariots for those who use those exits to take them home because once you take the exit, there is no turning back.

Along this beautiful highway, there are thick bushes, deserts, rivers, lakes, mountains, and valleys. People get lost in those bushes where they cannot be traced. Demons and other evil spirits await you in the bushes. They tend to take one away from righteousness. That is why people become confused, disappointed, and discouraged by losing hope in life, because they have no start nor end once they go astray. Sometimes the lost ones go through deserts, valleys, or mountains and become tired or weary in life. Sometimes someone may reach a river that is flooded, with no bridge. Perhaps there are huge snakes and crocodiles waiting, with their mouths wide open. Behind them, demons are following, changing into different fearful creatures.

When one reaches this point, one becomes mentally confused, aggressive, or violent. At this point, one tends to lack humanity and becomes desperate in the sense that one becomes capable of doing any inhuman act.

That is why Jesus was sent by God to come into the world to find and seek those who are lost in the bushes. Jesus, in his teachings, talked about the lost sheep. Jesus also came to be the light to the world for those who are in darkness. He is the light that will lead others back to the road of happiness and righteousness once again. Today, only those who want to remain in darkness will do so; otherwise, Jesus is there to help us. The angels are all over, serving those ready to be served.

Life is a game that you lose to die or win to live. God has made it very simple, but we complicate it so much, so that we fail to understand the true meaning of life at large. Those who embrace Jesus as their helper become, once again, God's chosen people and His best friends. God is ready to renew their strength, as He promised. God's joy becomes their strength, but those who reject Him receive only the spirit of confusion and disturbance. God's will is for everyone to finish the journey of life using the righteous path, but unfortunately we die due to our ignorance and iniquities.

Then I saw people grouped into three groups. The first group had only a few people. Those were the righteous people who agreed to be persecuted and to suffer in the name of Jesus Christ. They had refused to bow down to idols and worshipped their God throughout their lives, no matter the circumstances. They were rejected; humiliations and suffering were their daily bread. The king Jesus had greater rewards for them. They were crowned and dressed in white-cream robes. They were welcomed into the kingdom of God without question. They were given authority and power to judge the people of all nations. They were made to be the rulers of the world with Jesus. In other words, they were ordained to be judges of the world, to be kings, and to reign with Jesus as the king of kings for a thousand years.

The second group had also only a few people. Those were the people who knew nothing or had not yet heard about God, mostly because of their inability to function well. They could not differentiate their left hand from their right hand. Those people would not be judged at all. They would be welcomed in the house of the Lord. They would be given their reward, though they were not as gorgeous as the first group.

The third group contained the majority of people—about 85% of the world's population. Those were the people who claimed that they could see, but they were blind. Those were the people who claimed to be knowing God, doing God's will, and loving him with all their hearts, but they did not. Their cases were undetermined. They were told to line up in front of each judge or king. What surprised me was that some of them acknowledged that they did not belong to the kingdom of God. They were given their rewards accordingly. Their sins haunted them, and they could see themselves in the reflection of all the things that they had done. Some of them qualified to enter into the kingdom of God, and they were about 25% of the total number of people in the third group. This group and the second group were put together. But what amazed me was that all of these people had their names written in the Book of Life.

Then, I heard Jesus asking for another book, the Book of Remembrance, where all the promises were recorded. This book contained the prayer requests of the righteous people requesting salvation for people who were not righteous. All those names were read, and those people were selected from the third group from those who were left. They were about 25% of the total number of the third group. They were saved from the anger of God. They were allowed to enter into the kingdom of God and given white robes but no other rewards. Therefore, not all people will be equal in Holy City. Some will be kings, some rich or poor, in the Holy City; the choice is yours today.

In the Bible, John 9:39–41, Jesus said, *"I came to this world to judge, so that the blind should see and those who see should become blind."* Some *Pharisees who were there with him heard him say this and asked him, "Surely you do not mean that we are blind, too?" Jesus answered, "If you were blind, then you would not be guilty; but since you claim that you can see, this means that you are still guilty."* God will not judge us, but we will judge ourselves because we claim that we know and we are righteous. If we acknowledge that we are blind and sinners, then there is no judgment upon us.

Salvation

Salvation comes from God. God created the world and all those who inherited it with the purpose that they would live forever. He did not create the world for them to perish, but sins altered the will of God. Sins resulted in the death of the physical body. But the soul does not die. After understanding man's mind, God concluded that He would not compete with human beings. Therefore, He would never bring destruction to the world except on the last day of the judgment. He set aside a Day of Judgment so that all that is an abomination will be destroyed by everlasting fire.

Many of us do not understand the meaning of the word salvation. Salvation, in simple terms, means that all those who will come out victorious, or will persevere, shall be saved from the wrath of God. Salvation is a vision of what will happen in the day of the Lord. Those who walk with the Lord will have a vision of salvation when God comes on that day. The day of the Lord is the day when the world will receive its judgment. God will pour His anger onto the world and only those who have His mark, those who have washed their wedding gowns in the blood of the lamb, shall be saved.

According to Daniel 3:8–30, *King Nebuchadenezzar threw Shadrach, Meshach, and Abednego into the blazing furnace; the blaze had no power to consume them. A fourth person was seen in the midst of those three friends. They had been tied with ropes, but they were seen walking about in the fire together with the fourth person. The fourth person was the Son of God. The same thing will happen on the day of the Lord. All those who are called by His name or who call upon His holy name shall be saved from the wrath of God and the fire will have no power over them.*

The world will receive three judgments. The first judgment will be because of the sins that were committed by our first parents. The second will be because the world did not show hospitality to Jesus but made him suffer and later crucified him on the cross. The third will be because of a collection of sins that all individuals have committed.

Those who have established good relationships with God have the vision of salvation. Therefore, to be saved means that one is trying to live according to God's standard. It does not mean that one cannot make mistakes in life or commit sins; we are all human beings until we leave our dirty bodies. We fall and sometimes run short of God's glory, though we are committed to doing good. But God teaches those who are His and corrects them with love and kindness. Once their mistakes are corrected, their sins are remembered no more. That is one of the reasons why the truly righteous suffer—because their mistakes are corrected on the spot or even before they are done. Those whose mistakes and sins have accumulated will be judged on the last day of the Lord. Remember, God is just and therefore we do not expect Him to overlook some mistakes or sins. Punishment must be received for any mistake or sin committed, despite our relationship with Him. But the method of punishment is different. Some receive punishment and then correction instantly, while others wait until the day of the judgment. Until they recognize and appreciate God in their lives by repenting their sins, their names *will not* be written in the book of life, or their names *will* be written in the book of life.

Therefore, do what pleases God and walk with the Lord. Praise him and worship him by day and night forever. Establish a good relationship with God and live a holy and righteous life. Acknowledge the presence of God and that Jesus died to set us free and to reconcile man with God. Truly, you shall be saved when Jesus comes with the power and glory on that day.

THE COMING OF JESUS CHRIST

The purpose of the coming of Jesus Christ for the second time is to prepare the harvest or the bride (the church) for his Father. Jesus and the Holy Ghost will be given the authority to condemn and uproot any tree that does not bear fruit. They will come with the battalion from heaven to judge the world. Jesus, who came to the world as a poor man, who humbled himself, for he was born in a manger, will come with the Power, Glory, and Authority of God. He will come with the anger of his Father to avenge Him. People of all races and tribes will try to run away from His presence. They will try death, but death will have no power. Those who belong to Him will be happy because their day of salvation will have arrived. They will rush to welcome their king and bridegroom in the sky.

Jesus will come to judge the world. He will separate the good from the evil. All those who are good, who have lived according to God's word, will be ready to be taken home. Those who are evil and wrong doers will be thrown into a lake of fire. The Devil himself is an angel of fire. He will stand at the center, and the fire will spread from him to form a lake of fire. He will consume all the sinners who belong to him because the Devil has no friend, but the Devil himself will not burn. He will laugh at you because he misleads you. The Devil is not and will never be your friend. The choice is yours, but if you agree to be deceived by the Devil, you will cry alone and you will not be able to blame him. The heaven and the earth shall pass away together with all those who will have been thrown into the lake of fire. They will disappear in the eyes of the Lord and God will remember them no more. Their records will be destroyed, and this will be the second death.

Jesus will reign for a thousand years. During this time, Jesus will teach us how to behave in the house of the King, in the presence of the almighty God. He will teach people the true praising and worshipping of God. It will be a time for preparation. Those who are victorious will reign with Jesus. Jesus will give them a shepherd's rod and the same authority he received from God. After that, he will take the righteous home, where God will be waiting for them. They will be called God's children, and God will be their God. There will be only one language in the new Holy City. God Himself will not meet anyone or anything that is not clean. Only those who are holy indeed shall see God.

Rewards

According to Revelation 22:12, Jesus said, " *Behold, I am coming soon! I will bring my rewards with me, to give each one according to what he has done.*" This means we will not be rewarded the same. Here on earth we talk about the five gifts of the Holy Spirit. But Jesus has seven rewards that are kept for those who will emerge triumphant, apart from the eternal life that will be given to all those who will be called the children of the most high king. According to the book of the Revelation 2 and 3, those gifts are:

- *To those of us who win the victory, Jesus will give the right to eat the fruit of the tree of life that grows in the Garden of God.*

- *To those of us who are faithful to God, even if it means death, Jesus will give life as a prize of victory. Surely those of us who win the victory will not be hurt by the second death.*

- *To those of us who win the victory, Jesus will give some of the hidden manna. He will also give each of us a white stone on which is written a new name that no one knows except the one who receives it. This is true because in a vision, a stone that was round and had flames of fire was put in me. I was told to receive a new name. The name was written on top but because of the flames of fire it was only I who could read it. The new name I received is a secret between God and me.*

- *To those of us who win the victory, who continue to the end to do what Jesus wants, he will give the same authority that he received from our Father: He will give us authority over the nations, to rule them with an iron rod and to break them to pieces like clay pots. He will give us the morning star because Jesus is the morning star of the Holy City. Together we shall be the lights in the Holy City of God, and that is why no sun or moon will be needed. The morning star is seven times brighter than our sun.*

- *To those of us who win, we will walk with Jesus, clothed in white, because we are worthy to do so. And Jesus will not remove our names from the book of the living. In the presence of our heavenly Father God and His angels, Jesus will declare openly that we belong to Him. Amen.*

- *To those of us who are victorious, Jesus will make us pillars in the temple of our God and we will never leave it. Jesus will write on us the name of our God, the new Jerusalem, which will come down out of heaven from our God. Jesus will also write his new name on us.*

- *To those of us who win the victory, Jesus will give the right to sit beside him on his throne, just as he has been victorious and now sits by our heavenly Father on His throne.*

As for that group that belongs to Satan, those liars who claim that they are children of God, but they are not, Jesus will make them come and bow down at our feet. They will all know that Jesus who died for our sins is alive and he loves us.

Who will receive the above rewards?

According to the Bible, in the book of Matthew 5:3-11, those who qualify are:-

- Those of us who know that we are spiritually poor. The kingdom of heaven will belong to us.

- Those of us who mourn, because the world treats us in a merciless, scornful and bitter way. God will bring comfort to us all.

- Those of us who are humble. We will receive what God has promised.

- Those of us whose greatest desire is to do what God requires. God will satisfy us fully.

- Those of us who are merciful to others. God will be merciful to us.

- Those of us who are pure in heart. We will see God.

- Those of us who work for peace. God will call us His children.

- Those of us who are persecuted because we do what God requires. The kingdom of heaven belongs to us.

Happy are we when people insult us and persecute us and tell all kinds of evil lies against us, because we are true followers of God. Our reward that God has kept for us in heaven is great.

Our rewards will not be based on the gifts of the Holy Spirit but on the fruits of the Holy Spirit. So, my brothers and sisters, be wise. Stop fighting for things that have no reward.

Gifts and Fruits of the Holy Spirit

Jesus is the tree of life and we are the branches. A tree bears fruit on its branches. God is the taproot of the tree. The Holy Spirit of God carries the nutrients from the root to the branches for the branches to bear fruit, and the branches is all those who have accepted Jesus Christ.

Each branch or individual must bear nine different types of fruit. These are of the Holy Spirit and it is such fruit, such attributes, that each of us needs in order to be complete and to be with Jesus Christ: *love, joy, peace, patience, kindness, goodness, faithfulness, humanity* and *self-control*. That is why Jesus said that those who belong to him shall be identified by the fruit that they bear, which is meant to be eaten by other people of the world, Christians and non-Christians alike. Without bearing this fruit, one cannot claim to be a true follower of Jesus.

A good Christian should evaluate himself and find out whether he is bearing all nine types of fruit. If not, which one is he not bearing, so that he can ask God to provide him with the right nutrients? For failure to bear fruit, you will be thrown into the lake of fire. Remember it is said that the axe and the fire are kept near to cut and burn the tree that does not bear fruit. Surely, if you are Christian but not bearing fruit, are you still a part of the tree? Are you getting nutrients from God through the Holy Spirit? You do not have to wait until you are told whether you qualify to enter into heaven. The basic qualities of entering into heaven are simply that one must bear the nine types of fruit, live those attributes with all your being, to the best of your capability.

When Christians come together who live in the truth of these nine types, they are able to interact and worship together; God gives them tools through the Holy Spirit. Those tools help them to do the work of the Lord in the field. They are able to correct, feed, encourage, uplift, and prune one another. One person has a hymn, another one has a teaching, another one a revelation from God, another a message in strange tongues and another one the explanation of what is said in strange tongues according to 1 Corinthians 26. Those tools, in other word, are called the gifts of the Holy Spirit.

When two or more people come together they form a church, because it is hard to find all five attributes in one person. It is not essential that we must have all of them. In fact, we cannot boast, even if we have all of them, because it is God who works in us. Actually, God can use anything, including stones with the gift of the Holy Spirit, but He cannot use stones to bear the fruit of the Holy Spirit. For instance, He can use a stone to speak in strange tongues or to explain them, but He cannot use stones to give love or to be kind to people. Many Christians are fighting and competing to have the gifts instead of bearing the fruit. It is better to bear fruit.

There are so many questions that bother so many people today. Is it possible for God to use someone who does not belong to Him? Why does God use people in a mighty way, yet the person does not belong to Him?

Yes, it is true that we do not need to be Christians to use the tools from the Holy Spirit. We are clay and the work of God's hands and He has the right to use anyone or anything in this world to glorify Him. That is why many Christians will be rejected from being used in a mighty way, because they do not bear any of the nine types of fruit from the sacred tree.

Those who bear fruit are the true children of God but those who use the tools without bearing fruit, without living in those attributes, are simply workers who go back to their homes after payment. For example, in an exam room you may find people who are not registered or qualified to take the exam. They are there to work for pay, but not to pass exams. They do not have to study to pass the exam, but they can be hired to watch students.

You can fast and pray to live in truth with the nine attributes of love, joy, peace, patience, kindness, goodness, faithfulness, humanity and self-control—so that God can fill you with His fullness, but you do not have to pray for the gifts, because they are automatic.

When two or more meet, God knows their needs and therefore God meets their needs through the Holy Spirit, by providing them with tools that are required for their work at that time. The choice is yours today; you can choose to bear fruit or to just use the tools. But I would advise you to bear fruit because God has several rewards waiting for you. The true church of Christ is not a building or just any gathering; it is where and when two or more who bear the different nine attributes gather together.

Watch Out

Sometimes the Holy Spirit leaves for a day or even a couple of days and then we feel empty or weak. It does not mean that we have sinned or God is not with us. But we should be extremely careful because that is the time the enemy is on the lookout. In just a blink of an eye we can find ourselves doing things that do not please God. What happens is that when the Holy Spirit returns and find out that we have sinned or that we have invited an enemy into our hearts, then she does not enter into our hearts again. Be cautious for such moments.

My brothers and sisters, if you forgive others the wrongs they have done to you, surely our heavenly Father will also forgive you. But if you do not forgive others, then our heavenly Father will not forgive you too. Confess your sins and give them up; then God will show you His love, mercy and favor. You will not go to heaven if you try to hide them.

Always obey His laws and you will be happy. If you are stubborn, He will find your prayers too hateful to hear and you will be ruined.

God bless you.

Amen.

Heaven, the Holy Place of God,
this is where I desire to be.

My sweet heart, I have a dream for you, a dream to help persevere all the way through. My sweet heart stands in the promises of God, the promises that will never fail and they will help you to overcome all the obstacles. I have seen God's wonders and because I believe in Him I can take the future. The destination makes it valuable to press on through the darkest moment in life. I believe when I know my time has come I will cross the river of death to my beautiful destination to live with my sweet Father because He loves me.

BIOGRAPHY

CHARLES ELEPHANT

Charles Elephant was born and brought up in a beautiful town, Mukurwe-ini, Nyeri in Kenya. His real name is Charles Njogu, but Njogu means Elephant in his language. He completed a Master's degree in International Finance and Economics at Brandeis University in 2003. He is completing another Master's Degree in Science at New York University. He came to the United States in 2001 and lived in Waltham, Massachusetts, but most recently resides in Newark, New Jersey.

He came to know God and understand His ways in the early 1990s. Since then, his life has been changed completely. At first, he was confused and bothered because he could not understand his mission and his life seemed nothing but chaos. He wanted to hear directly from God and learn more from Him. He knew that if there was a God, surely He had good stories to tell. He longed for those good stories day and night, until finally God heard his prayers and blessed him according to his heart's desire.

He is inspired most by this passage from *Isaiah 57: 14-21*. The Lord says:

"Let my people return to me. Remove every obstacle from their path! Build the road, and make it ready! I am the high and holy God, who lives forever. I live in a high and holy place, but I also live with people who are humble and repentant, so that I can restore their confidence and hope. I gave my people life, and I will not continue to accuse them or be angry with them forever. I was angry with them because of their sin and greed, so I punished them. But they were stubborn and kept on going their own way. I have seen how they acted, but I will heal them, and I will comfort those who mourn. I offer peace to all, both near and far! I will heal my people. But the evil men are like the restless sea, whose waves never stop rolling in, bringing filth and muck. There is no safety for sinners."

It is his humble desire to tap into more knowledge and wisdom from God in order to teach His children. His heart's desire is to write more books and to record music of Praise and Worship.

Contacts: cnn546@yahoo.com or www.echoesofheaven.org

Printed in the United States
50238LVS00005B/28-99